(continued from front flap)

tant teachers of the child, precisely what they should teach and how often seems to raise an insuperable problem. With warmth and verve Antoinette Becker narrates her own experiences in explaining the meaning of God, Jesus, life and death, sexual love, friendship, honesty, and the sacraments to her six growing children.

In simple and direct dialogue with her children, Antoinette Becker is never domineering, arbitrary, or pedantic. The more delicate or difficult questions are never thrust aside or left only partially answered. Mrs. Becker stresses again and again that children's questions are normal healthy expressions of their desire to know. The deepest mysteries of existence and of religion are broached in a candid and reverent way that reflects the close bond of mother and child. The freshness of this book, its unadorned charm, and its deep educational meaning flow from the author's ability to capture, touch, and clarify the inner world of the child through experienced love and understanding. It is a book that every parent will want to read, reflect upon, and apply to his own family life.

In the words of Sidney Callahan the great value of Children Ask About God and Everything is "its ability to inspire. Its simplicity and integrity can renew despairing adults to new efforts."

CHILDREN ASK ABOUT GOD
AND EVERYTHING

CHILDREN ASK ABOUT GOD AND EVERYTHING

A Book for Mothers and Teachers

Antoinette Becker

HERDER AND HERDER

St. Mary's College Library,
Winona, Minnesota

1966
HERDER AND HERDER NEW YORK
232 Madison Avenue, New York 10016

Original edition: *Kinder Fragen nach Gott,*
Matthias-Grunewald-Verlag, Mainz, 1962.
Translation by Sister M. Dolores Sablone, R.S.M.

Nihil obstat: Patrick A. Barry
            Censor Librorum
Imprimatur: Patrick C. Brennan
            Vicar General, Diocese of Burlington
            November 12, 1965

The *Nihil obstat* and *Imprimatur* are official declarations that a book or
pamphlet is considered to be free of doctrinal or moral error. No impli-
cation is contained therein that those who have granted the *Nihil obstat*
and *Imprimatur* agree with the contents, opinions, or statements expressed.

Library of Congress Catalog Card Number: 66–13078
© 1966 by Herder and Herder, Incorporated
Manufactured in the United States of America

Contents

375.2
Db39

69113

CONTENTS

Foreword

Speaking together is the most uniquely human activity. The ability to communicate through language sets man apart from the animals and gives him dominion over creation. Only through the possession of language can men, women, and children realize the spiritual and aesthetic resources of humankind. If words mirror reality, they also create reality; we are even told that "In the beginning was The Word . . ." Certainly, the beginning of each child's life centers around words, which give him the gift of language, introduce him to his culture, and shape his views of God and the world.

In Western society the parents' voice in the home shapes the child's earliest years. By the time a child enters the public society of school or church he is already formed. The mass media of television and radio may counter the family's influence (much as did the old village-centered communal society), but since parents control these sources of outside influence they retain primary responsibility for their children. It is both an exhilarating challenge and a dread-full trust to raise a child and teach him what he should know.

Surely, most Christian parents tremble before this awesome task. It is such a subtle undertaking to convey the Christian faith and at the same time inspire the child to love and obey Christ. Any easy reliance upon God and the Church to do it all is a dangerous presumption. At the other extreme a too Freudian faith in the power of the unconscious is an equally irresponsible retreat: "Oh well, it doesn't matter what we do or say, what

7

we believe and what we are will do the job." If we do not care enough to try to convey verbally the faith that is ours, then we have already sent a rather strong message to our children.

But granting parental efforts and good will, American parents will still face many difficulties in instructing their children. A subtle problem for many parents lies in the prevailing Anglo-Saxon reticence regarding intimate private matters of prayer and faith. In American social circles there is a great reluctance to discuss one's religion or religious experience. Many parents find it easier to instruct their children about the sexual facts of life than the spiritual truths of the faith. American individualism and emphasis upon the freedom and privacy of one's faith not only retards the Christian social conscience, but handicaps unselfconscious parental instruction.

Things are not made any easier by the general anti-authoritarian cast to our culture (generally a healthy characteristic). No one tells the individual what to do or what to believe— parents least of all. Parental authority is weakened not only because the society does not reënforce it, but because parents cannot believe in it themselves. The intense change and mobility in our society often means that parents themselves had to disregard their parents in order to develop. Many of the present generation of committed Christians are so despite their own parents' agnosticism or indifference so prevalent in the twenties. And many Roman Catholics emerging from a hyper-authoritarian paternalism full of abuses cannot help but be wary of their own assumption of authority. Moreover, many of these newly educated Catholic laymen are not yet confident in the taking of initiative and responsibility in religious matters. We must struggle to overcome our timidities.

Of course, another formidable obstacle in instructing our children lies in the hectic chaotic quality of current family living. There is little time to talk of anything, or read anything, let alone time for prayer and Scripture reading. Nor is this tension solely the result of television addiction or mindless overactivity in community affairs. Many of the disintegrating forces are beyond the control of the family. A suitable dwelling for children can usually only be found far from the father's work so that more often than not the whole burden of raising the family rests upon the mother alone. It is a rare family who have any kinfolk or hired help in the household.

Since most educated American Catholics have been faithful to the Church's ban upon contraceptives, many, many families will have children in a very short time-span (three in three years is a commonplace). Until the older children become old enough to help with the small ones, a large family raised with high child-rearing standards requires tremendous energy and time. The leisure for conversation is lost in the struggle to dress, feed, bathe, and bed the family. Civilized family meals can become almost impossible for years at a time.

In light of all of these special problems in American culture, can Mrs. Becker's book, written in a European setting, be of any use to us? Her situation is one which is uncommon in America, with grandmother in residence, household help, and an established cultural tradition to reënforce her teaching. Solidity, respect for authority, and organized households characterize the European cultural milieu in which she writes. Her children sound delightful, but much more willing and docile than our skeptical, hyperactive American children. The young Beckers have their problems, but on the whole they seem too good to be

9

true. This is due, probably, not only to cultural differences, but to their mother's rare gifts of character. She is unusual, they are unusual, it is not a typical family. Once that is granted, then one can go on without too much discouragement and aspire towards these high standards.

For this is the great value of this book for mothers and teachers, its ability to inspire. Its simplicity and integrity can renew mildly despairing adults to new efforts. I found the meditations upon motherhood particularly moving, perhaps since I also have five sons and one cherished daughter, but also, I think, because there is something very real here common to all mothers. Surely, the painful thoughts of the concentration-camp children have troubled more mothers than Mrs. Becker and myself. Also the insights into the joys of birth (though sounding sentimental) are very real. The joys, anxieties, and sorrows of parenthood are so intense that they may often sound sentimental or melodramatic to the outsider.

But what of the specific models for religious instruction given here? The tradition of instructing through presenting conversations has antecedents all the way back through Erasmus to Plato. What is lost in explication and efficiency is compensated for by spirit and flavor. We can savor these dialogues and use what we can when we can. The fact that they presuppose a subtle and intimate relationship with one's children, a "prepared environment" beyond most families, can also be instructive. Above all, I admire their reverent yet straightforward quality. My favorite example of Mrs. Becker's approach is her response to her son's right action under stress: "Yes, but Jesus would say to you, 'David, you have understood me; I'm in you and you're in me.'"

SIDNEY CORNELIA CALLAHAN

A Note to Mothers

THIS book comes from pages of my diary and notes. It reproduces talks which I have had with my own and with other children, and it will help those disposed to talk to children about God, especially parents.

These talks are for children from their earliest years to their ninth. Parents should not think complacently that priests and teachers will give children the religious education and training they need. This is the first duty of parents. They are the ones who lay the foundation. On them depends the development or stunting of a child's sensitivity to respond. They are the ones who help the child unfold and they are the ones who can stand in the way of a child's natural progress. Parents develop a child's power to withstand, his vigor and sense of reality. In their religious instruction teacher and priest build on the work of the parents.

In these talks the Church year and parts of holy Scripture are treated without any claim to the last word; needless to say, this book is not meant to be a full catechetical course in religious instruction. I have wanted merely to point out examples of how in these our times we can talk to children about God. The examples are related to the great feasts of the Church year, to various texts of the Old and New Testaments, as well as to the sacraments and commandments which the child encounters in the early years of his or her life. In connection with this I have added a first instruction on the mysteries of life. Some of the texts in the Scriptures must be related to the child's life, explained, and talked over. Others should only be read to the child. I have given examples of both. A child can absorb a great many things which he cannot as yet grasp with the reason but which gradually become more comprehensible as time goes on. Knowledge unfolds in a repeated experience. Education and religion constitute a whole in the life of the family, and for a child religion is an integral part of his life which he shares with his parents. Hence, I have left the words of the children unchanged in their childish simplicity.

Not only do parents speak to their children about God, but God also speaks to parents out of the mouths of their children. Children ask about God. They give a calm expression to terrible things, yet they know how to take the big things for granted. We should never become weary of listening to them and of telling them what we ourselves have experienced.

Each parent has his own way of talking to his or her child, therefore the examples given in this book are not presented for imitation merely. They point out how talks can be carried on with children about God in their personal lives, in everything they do, in their own religious growth.

The index is in no way complete. It is meant only to be an aid in finding important names and subjects.

Antoinette Becker

Letter to Isabel

My dear child,
Andrew, your oldest brother, is now seventeen years old, Peter
just fifteen, and Manuel twelve. David is almost seven and
Daniel, whom we still call the baby, celebrates his third birthday
in a few days. You, my only daughter among five brothers, are
now ten.

I have taken notes on all of the children because I was afraid
that with the passing of time I might forget the questions they
asked and the things they said.

When you were born I decided to put a book together for you
which you could perhaps use later in the education of your own
children. Things are not arranged in it in strictly chronological
order. Sometimes I tell a story about Andrew and Peter when
they were six and seven years old, sometimes about them when
they were twelve and thirteen. Don't let this confuse you. The
memory of their early childhood is still with me. I am sure every
mother has this experience even when her children are grown up.

With the arrival of each new child came other stories, and,
above all, new answers. I have developed too in the course of the
years, and the problems have become more embracing and
deeper. Knowledge makes one not only wiser and more secure,
but it also calls forth frighteningly new questions. In spite of
the circumspection which an acquired understanding afforded,
my disposition did not always show itself with you. This cir-

13

cumspection should have manifested itself in greater patience, in more attentive listening, in answers which were direct but not hasty. May the attempts I have made here and the care I took help you, dear Isabel.

Is it because Adam and Eve
didn't do what God said?

Before the birth of the child. Does it hurt, Mommy? Children and the unborn child. A natural explanation. Telling about natural birth. The child and formal prayer. What are disciples? The Christmas story. The joy before Christmas. Christmas gifts. Anxiety over the unborn child. Birth. The father at the birth of the child. A mother's first prayer with her child. The "older" children and the "new" baby. The child's capacity to love. Renunciation out of love. The foundation of a genuine union with God. Creation. There was light at first. The child within the mother. How is a baby born? Giving a correct and truthful answer.

THIS morning Andrew came to me as I sat in my room sewing.

"Mommy, do you think that the baby will be coming pretty soon?"

"Some time during the day I shall be going to the hospital, Andrew. I think that the baby might come today."

"Will it hurt, Mommy?"

"Oh, you know, it will be hard work, but *hurt?* That isn't quite the right word."

"Does it hurt Mitzi when kittens come out of her?"

15

"Well, yes, in a way. But with mothers it's different . . ."

"Is it because Adam and Eve didn't obey God? You told us that they didn't do what God said." And then he raised his little hand and looked quite prophetic as he announced, "You know, after that they knew what hot was and what cold was. They knew what hurt and what was bad. They were afraid and so the animals became angry." "Mommy," he said, and he kissed me, "I'll be careful." At the same time he stroked my body gently. "That is the baby. It is dark inside, but it is just like a little house. I was there once. You told me so. Mommy, don't worry. If anything happens to you, I'll take care of the new baby and my brothers along with my own children!"

Good little Andrew with all of his small six years! Peter's good honest face now appeared. He had come in to see me, chubby little hands outstretched. Andrew stood up and placed himself like a wall between Peter and me. "Look out for the baby," he said full of business. "It might come today."

"You know, Mommy," he said softly, "Peter can't really understand. He is too small."

"I'm not small," rebelled Peter. "I'm four and that much," and he bent a little finger in demonstration. "The baby is inside Mommy now. But when she opens her mouth and calls him, he'll be right here!"

Andrew keeps silence. I hug Peter. He already knows quite a bit about the mystery of life but his knowledge will grow gradually the way Andrew's did.

"As long as I'm still here, let's tell the Christmas story again. Andrew, you begin," I said.

16

He did so very beautifully and slowly.

"Now it is my turn," Peter calls out. "Glory to God up in the clouds."

"No, in the highest!"

"Isn't it nicer to say it my way?"

"It's very nice, but we want to say it the way it is in the Gospel, the way the apostle Luke said it."

"What is an apostle?"

"Someone Jesus loved, someone who went around the world baptizing people and telling them about Jesus."

"Then what are disciples, Mommy?"

"Disciples are friends of Jesus."

All of a sudden Andrew starts up with, "It's almost Christmas and the crib is coming and the star, the tree, and the lights!"

"And the presents," Peter adds prosaically.

"Yes, the presents because of the joy of the holy night. We want to make people happy."

"The night can't be holy. Only people are holy. Am I people?" Peter asks. "Am I holy?"

"The night is also holy," I explain to them. "Everything about this night was holy. Everything was connected with God. Just imagine! The redeemer was born." Then we were interrupted because Manuel came in. He is only seventeen months old.

"He always does that just when we're talking," grumbles Andrew.

"But you wanted to take care of him along with your own children if anything happened to me. Aren't I supposed to depend on you . . . ?"

17

"Come, Manuel," says Andrew. "You can say *Amen* at the end. You don't understand what it is all about but that's all right."

Yes, Andrew is right. It is all right. It makes no difference. We must all believe in the power of grace.

This evening I had a few pains. I sat very still. Dear God, let my child come into the world well in mind and body. If it must be otherwise, give me the help to accept it and to bear it. I trust in you but my anxiety keeps returning. Then the child moved in me and I was consoled. These last days it has been very still because it has had less and less room. But each of its movements is a great reassurance.

Isabel! You came into the world tonight at five minutes before one, my first little daughter. And how dear you looked, —a real person with a tiny perfect little face, round, large, and well-formed. You yourself will one day be able to understand the gratitude which overwhelms mothers when a child is born. The Gospel is right. "When a woman has given birth to a child she thinks no more on her anguish (*labores,* hard work, Isabel, not pain!) because of the joy that a person has come into the world." I was so full of gratitude that everything went well. Now you are lying beside me, a new person, living and breathing. There is an immediate bond with God and the one who has given life to a new being. Your father was such a comfort to me tonight. He helped me with his unshakable confidence. Later he held you in his arms, put you back into the crib, and made the sign of the cross lightly on your forehead. I did the same and afterwards I held your tiny hand in mine and prayed with you. I felt the strong indissoluble tie which binds us together. I did the same with the other children in the family. When they were only a few months old I noticed that they waited for this time especially in the evening. I remember how Andrew twined his little fingers together when he was hardly eleven months old and since he could not talk yet, he merely said dadeldadeldadelda. I remember how he looked up at me beaming and bright. Peter said lately that we really don't know when we began to pray.

Today the three boys came to visit us. How excited they were and how different their reactions! Manuel was the happiest because Isabel was cute when she cried. Andrew wrinkled his nose and wanted to know, "Does she always screech like that?" Peter just said matter-of-factly, "She's alive," and then he wanted to drink the red currant juice which was on the table.

"She's alive, Andrew."

"But she's crying . . ."

"Is she real?"

"See for yourself!"

"Can I really love her?"

These were hard words for me. "But I thought you would all be happy," I said. How good it was that I could nip their jealousy in the bud. Naturally, I had to hide my own disappointment. "Don't you think she's dear, Andrew? She's so small

19

and yet so perfectly formed. It's good that you can protect her later. When we're home again, maybe you could sleep in her room sometime, and you too, Peter." With that the children became happy again.

"Oh, she's looking at me. She's laughing!"

In reality you were looking at some unknown object and making a wry little mouth.

"She knows me already," Andrew exclaimed.

"Me, too!" With that you were adopted, accepted, and above all you found a place in their hearts.

Be careful when your children show jealousy, Isabel. Don't become immediately alarmed about it. Take particular pains to see what the difficulty is. Restore command and then heal the wounds of the child or untangle the twisted thread of hurt feelings.

How energetically you drink, Isabel, how busy you are! And afterwards how happy! Your sense of perception grows from day to day. When you cry I soothe you with comforting words and it seems to me that you stop at the sound of my voice.

You stop crying. This stopping of crying when you hear my voice is really like a renunciation of something, a giving up something out of love, one might say. This is a first step in your education. It is the first step in the development of your conscience. I read a lovely book about all of this, and this evening I talked it over with your father. The author thinks that a child needs to be able to love. And whether or not a child has this capacity appears in her ability to give up something for the sake of someone she loves, that is, the mother, just as you are now

20

learning to wait until I pick you up to nurse you. I read this from the book to your father: "Probably the most decisive thing is the training of a child's capacity to love. When a child loves an older person he loves this person not only as someone who moves about in his world but also as his model. A child gives expression to this fact by its outward behavior. It loves the moral demands made by this person and it is motivated to imitation." I don't want ever to forget this. I want to educate you all in this power to love because I consider it to be the foundation of the love of God, the very basis of religion. For *religio* means to unite with the ultimate, with God.

Today, quite unexpectedly, Peter said to me as I held him on my lap and kissed him, "I'm praying that you will have a lot of milk for Isabel. I mean, I'm praying that you can nurse her," he explained.

The coming baptism was keeping the children busy.

"Will they really put her in the water?"

"No, Peter."

"Isabel is already clean. Why does she have to be washed in church?"

"Look, Peter, I have already told you about paradise. God created light first."

"I know that," says Andrew. "God waved his hand and said *light* in his mind and then the light came out of the darkness."

"When did God discover himself?" Peter wants to know.

"God was always there. He has no beginning and he has no end."

"But didn't he have even a little beginning?"

"No!" Andrew is completely upset. "God is, He always was. If he had invented himself he would have had to be there to exist in order to invent himself, wouldn't he?"

"Maybe he came just a tiny bit out of nothing," and Peter makes a small comical gesture with his hand.

Then Andrew asks in a clipped and imperious manner, "And who discovered the nothing?" Good little Peter replies ever so meekly, "He must have come at least a little bit out of nothing." But he is no longer so secure.

"I wanted to talk to you about creation," I try again. "You know that light was created on the first day, the sky on the second day, the world with everything that grows in it and the stars . . ."

"Oh, sun, moon, and stars, I love you so much," breaks in Peter. He is so sincere when he expresses his feelings that I often want to laugh, to smile, and to ponder. Let him express himself just as he sees it.

"And then the fish and the birds, the mammals and people . . ."

"Are people mammals?"

"Yes, but we don't say *mammals* when we talk about people. A human being, a mother, gives her child something to drink. She nurses the baby the way all animals do who bear their young and bring them into the world."

"Chickens don't do that," muses Andrew thoughtfully. "The eggs come and then the chicks slip out of them!"

22

"It's just the same with fish."

"But it's not the same with our cat, pussy! The kittens come out of her. They aren't pretty at first," says he matter-of-factly, "but later they are."

"But Isabel is pretty," Peter continues. "She was pretty the minute she came out of you. She even had hair on her head and she had such cute little cheeks and such pretty little feet. But they are always so curled up, not straight like mine. . . ."

"No, Peter, a little child makes himself very small when he lives in his mother. He draws up his little arms and feet close to his body. At first he is very small and then he grows a little bit more every day. After many months he is big enough to come into the world and to live in it without the protection of his mother."

"Did they have to cut your stomach?"

"No, Peter. A child comes into the world in the same way in which a hen lays an egg or the way kittens come from the mother cat."

"Then you have to be very careful when you have to go to the bathroom so that it won't come out."

"No, Peter. Next to this passage God made another one and this is where the baby comes from. The opening becomes bigger when the baby comes and after the baby is here it becomes small again. But we wanted to talk about people. God did not give the animals, particularly to the clever ones like the horse and to the less complicated ones like the worm, for example, what he gave only to human beings."

"A clock?" asks Peter. "I'd like a clock so much. . . ."

I sense that they have had enough. Peter wants to play now.

Andrew, however, makes a wry face. He would rather ask more questions.

The desire to know more, to investigate and to probe, is present. It is in all children beginning with the smallest ones. Of course, their questions are dependent on their temperament and maturity.

Often this curiosity to know hides behind a casual, inconsequential remark which disguises a question the child really wants to ask. We should give ear. We must learn to be sensitive to their little inaudible hints. Naturally, a child may express himself in very unusual language and with downright nonsense. But even in this case, I would say that one must be alert to detect the real problem behind the mask. There may be something lurking here which is overpowering the child.

Grown-ups should always be fair

You are going to marry some day, David. Explanation. Ties. Origin of life. The umbilical cord. Why cut it? Did you nurse me, too? Aggression occasioned by jealousy. Unimposed cleanliness. Difference between man and wife. Can one marry his sister? Is birth an illness? Birth is something very natural. Previous anxiety. Particular sensitivity during pregnancy. How can I really help my children? Impatience. The grandmother. The intoxication of Noah. Ham is cursed. Respect your father. Honor your parents.

"I'M always going to talk everything over with you, even when I'm big!"

"But when you're married you can't say to your wife, 'Today I'm going to Mommy to talk things over with her. . . .' "

"No, that won't do. Anyway, you will be dead. . . ."

"Not necessarily, but you will belong to your wife and you will be living with her in marriage. You will be taking your problems to her. You will help her. You will love her just as Papa and I love each other. . . ."

"I can't even imagine that, Mommy. I used to want to marry you and Isabel wanted to marry Papa, but now it's different."

"And you?"

"I don't want to any more, either. You have a husband and you're too old!"

"Yes, and anyhow, people can't marry their mother."

"But I love you so much, that I'd like to be inside you."

"That's not possible any more, darling."

"No more?"

"You were in me once. I've already told you about that. You were in my body, in the place where life begins. There you grew bigger, until the place became too small for you and there was no longer any room. You wanted to come out like a chick out of its eggshell. But I've told you about that, too."

"And what did you tell me about the cord?"

"It kept the two of us together."

"Why?"

"So that you could have food. You had to become fatter and bigger! The cord let the best that was in my blood flow into your body. When you were born you didn't need this any more and I didn't need it for you. And so the doctor just cut the cord which had united us."

"Where did he cut it?"

"Far enough away from your navel so that he wouldn't hurt you. You cried and your little lungs began to breathe by themselves."

"Why by themselves?"

"Because as long as you were in me they were closed. But when you were separated from me you breathed like a self-dependent person with your own lungs."

"Were my eyes open when I was in you?"

"No, you kept your eyes tightly closed."

26

"So that is why Daniel blinked at first."

"Yes, that is why. He wasn't used to having his eyes open."

"And did I drink the way Daniel did?"

"Of course. You drank a long time from my breast."

"But now I don't want to anymore."

"No, it wouldn't even taste good now."

"I'm too big and besides I have teeth!"

"Yes, you need them to chew with. Here, take a bite of this pretty apple. Only a big boy can do that. A baby couldn't do it."

"A baby wets his diapers. . . ."

"Oh, yes, but after a year or so baby learns to sit on the potty. He is taught how to do this and sometimes it takes a long time."

"Did I learn quickly?"

"Yes, very quickly."

"But Daniel is taking a long time. He's dirty!"

"No, he just needs time."

"I would spank . . ."

"If I'd spanked you, it would not have taken less time. Andrew taught Isabel how."

"How old was he?"

"Seven years old. He always used to get Isabel and put her on the potty."

"But Isabel is a girl."

"Yes, she's already a little lady. By this time she has many little eggs in her body and you have the seeds of life to go with them. Later on a child will grow in one of these eggs when it meets the seed of life."

"I could marry Isabel."

"No, you can't do that. You would be too much alike and your children would have poor health."

"Besides, we quarrel too much!"

"You'll have to look for a woman you don't know. . . ."

"She can be like Isabel."

"Perhaps. Isabel will find a husband and her children will be your nieces and nephews. They'll call you Uncle David."

"I'm so happy!"

"Mommy," asks Isabel, "were you sick when I was born?"

"Sick? No, of course not!"

"But some people almost die."

"No, no. The mother must work and she must take care that the child comes into the world safely."

"But Mrs. Berger said, 'The poor woman, one child after the other. She's just about dead!'"

"That's what a lot of people say, but Mrs. Berger has never had children. I know different. When a mother nurses her baby there won't be another baby for a while. When you go up a mountain carrying a well-filled pack, all goes well. If you do this a second time, you're not quite so fresh. But if you do it a third time you become tired. Being tired, though, is not the same as being sick. A mother who has one baby after the other becomes tired. But Papa has taken a lot of the burden from me. He helps me to do the carrying. He takes the wash from me, sends me to bed early, and does whatever he can wherever he can."

"Were you worried, Mommy?"

"Worried? Yes, sometimes for the child. I wondered if the

baby would be well, if she would be able to see and hear; otherwise, I didn't worry. I was always very happy."

"But you cried when you read to us."

"Naturally, when a mother is expecting a new baby she is much more sensitive, more easily moved, more delicate, so that if she reads something sad, she feels it that much more."

"You read to us about the little boy who was treated so badly by his father and of how he put up with so much."

"But doesn't that make you sad?"

"Very. I keep thinking what if my father were like that. . . ."

"And I keep thinking of how I would have shielded the child if he had been mine."

"But when Daniel falls down, you tell us not to pick him up!"

"Because mother must also know how to make her children grow up strong. Look, Daniel doesn't cry any more when he falls down. He picks himself up, looks around to see if anyone is going to give him sympathy, and then he toddles off. But if you said *poor Daniel* what would happen?"

"He would cry and . . ."

"Would it do him any good?"

"No. I understand now."

"What would Andrew have gotten out of it if I had worried myself sick the time he had appendicitis? I had to control my own fears in order to give him comfort and reassurance. Do you understand? You will have to learn to think things over, to decide what really helps."

"But if our Rosie drops something, please don't tell me it would improve her knees to bend down and pick it up quickly."

Isabel laughed delightedly. "See, you can twist anything around this way and that."

Manuel comes in while we are talking.

"Grandmother is an old pair of garden shears," grumbled Manuel.

"Why, now?"

"Because she is always impatient if I am slow and she scolds me."

"But she surely has a right to say something if you . . ."

"And she drank tea with her mouth full," Manuel interrupts. "My mouth has to be empty before I can drink. . . ."

"Tell me, do you really think this whole business is so bad? Grandmother is old, sick, very brave, very good, and once in a while a bit unfair."

"Grown-ups should always be fair!"

"Why? They do try to be fair. Grandmother tries but her strength is gone. She thinks about your good. Just imagine how she worries when something goes wrong in the house or when something happens to you. How quiet she is about the wonderful gifts she gives!"

"But why is she so unfair when she's so good?"

"Why are you so naughty sometimes although I know you love me? Do you remember the story of Noah, the one who built the ark? What are the names of his sons?"

"Shem, Ham and Japheth."

"After the flood Noah and his sons cultivated the land which had become dry again. They planted vineyards and drank the juice of the grapes. Naturally, Noah didn't know that grape

30

juice if left standing changes into wine and that wine intoxicates if one takes too much. It was hot. Noah was thirsty and he drank several glasses of wine. Then he became very tired. His legs became shaky. He swayed over to his tent, lay down, and fell into a deep but restless sleep. All he had for a blanket was the large cloth which he used for a cloak. This cloth slipped off and Noah lay there without any clothes on. Ham, in the meantime, came into the tent and found his snoring father lying naked on the ground. He started to joke about it. Even more than this, he called his brothers to join the fun. Shem and Japheth listened to their brother but they walked backwards into their father's tent."

"Backwards?"

"Yes, backwards, so that they would not have to look into their father's face as he lay in a somewhat laughable position. They covered him over. Disrespect for parents was a terrible sin at that time. When Noah woke up he found out how Ham had behaved. He cursed his son and his descendants, but he blessed his other sons, especially Shem. Later Abraham came from the race of Shem. You see, Manuel, the pious Noah was intoxicated. He could do nothing about it. He was just plain intoxicated."

"That's terrible!"

"But for Shem and Japheth he was and remained their father whom they were supposed to respect. He should have been approached with reverence. There is a proverb among the sayings of King Solomon: 'May crows pick out and young eagles devour the eye which is contemptuous of its father or which finds an aging mother despisable.' Do you know what I mean, Manuel? Swallow these little unpleasantnesses. Think that grandmother is papa's mother, just as I am your mother. See how he helps her when she is difficult. I think she knows precisely when she has not been nice and that she suffers because of it. If she were to die, you would be the first to give everything to have her back in the house looking after things even if she were a bit grumpy about it."

After an hour Manuel came back beaming and a little embarrassed.

"Grandmother blew soap bubbles with me!"

"Just like that?"

"I cleaned her shoes and shined them."

Manuel seems to have understood the story of Noah.

What is a redeemer?

We rehearse the Christmas story. Amusing fantasies of a child.
Gestures at prayer. An overcharged child. Blasphemy. A child's
natural love of God. Advent. Coming home with Isabel. The
picture Bible. Children and the psalms. What is a redeemer?
Jesus the redeemer. The birth of Jesus. Descent into hell and
ascension into heaven. Christmas presents. Prayers which children
do not understand. The child and ritual.

ANDREW and Peter came to the hospital today. They wanted to
rehearse the Christmas story which they knew very well. To be
sure, Peter thought out a new detail when he was retelling what
the angel said. "Look and see! Don't be afraid of me!"

"Oh!" he added. "It rhymes!"

I had to laugh, especially when I looked at him. But I didn't
scold or moralize. I merely explained the words of the Scriptures
again.

Mrs. B., my neighbor, told me that she was worried about her
little four-year-old son who wants to stand and lift his hands
when he prays. "But I'm already trying to take that out of him!"

I advised her not to disturb the child. Let him stand with
small upraised arms like a priest, provided he is praying in
earnest. But after a while she should ask him to kneel for the

end. No coercion should be used. Prayer should not become a dull horrible affair which the child is forced into. The child is supposed to be happy. He is supposed to learn to "talk" with God.

Mrs. B. came to visit me again today. She said radiantly, "Max is very good now when he prays! He doesn't do foolish things any more." She had done what I had suggested and she was very proud.

This reminds me of a story about my godchild, Clement, who was five at the time. He had had an overdose of Bible stories and one evening he stated grimly, hands in his pockets, feet spread apart and looking sinister, "Tomorrow I'm going to roast your God." This is blasphemous language and shocking, certainly. But it would be wrong in such a case to say, "You naughty child. You are a disgrace to talk like that. Quick! Take it back. Ask pardon. Aren't you ashamed of yourself?" Such procedure only destroys a child's relation to his God. Clement had wise parents and they brought him back gently. How much harm they might have done to the child had they acted otherwise!

They omitted the evening reading for several days until Clement began to ask impatiently for it. During the day he suddenly explained that he didn't want to roast God any more. A few years later during a bombing raid on his home town, Clement happened to be in the church attending a class for religious instruction. When the attack subsided his parents ran to the basement of the church to find him. At first they could not find him. Then suddenly Clement came brightly running to them. He had been lightly wounded in the head but he was radiant. "I went back quickly into the church to see if the crucifix was safe but only the foot had been chipped," he said. The story speaks for itself.

I remember, too, the time that I found Andrew before the crucifix in my bedroom. He was just three and a half. He stood there, his forehead wrinkled under his curly head. His tiny little face was folded into lines and he was saying with a dark challenging look, "I'm saying, 'whoa!' to Jesus because I'm naughty. 'Whoa! gee up!' " I stood very still. He didn't see me. Then he lowered his voice and I heard him say, "Did you hear me, Jesus on the cross? Did you hear what I said? Maybe you didn't hear me. Maybe I didn't say it. I really didn't want to say it. I really didn't mean it. I was very, very naughty, dear Jesus."

I left quietly. He did not need me. In the evening all he said was, "I said something to Jesus today but I've explained it to him already. Andy was naughty today."

Coming home with eight-day-old Isabel! What a tiring but perfect day! My room was so beautifully arranged for me. On the bookcase in the corner was the Advent spray complete with star and a concealed ball and candles, —just the way it is done in my native country. Only much later did I learn how to make a wreath. The spray is put in my room each year, but "their" wreath hangs in the children's room.

"Read to us tonight and then everything will be the same again," says Peter as he goes for the picture Bible.

"This is our evening book," he says. "It is a picture book about God," adds Andrew.

Manuel can just say "pitty" and he pats the book.

Peter understands only a few things, but this story he knows exactly. "I know this story. This is Daniel. This is a lion and this is a lion and this is a lion. Those are the *Balonians* who are looking down to see if Daniel is changed into a lion because lions eat people . . . but not Daniel. Look, he's sitting there and laughing. No, he's thinking."

"I think he is praying," puts in Andrew. They agree on this and both are happy. All three were sitting on my bed, but you, Isabel, were lying in your little crib, and I read them that passage from the psalms: "I lift up my eyes to the mountains." Andrew already knows what a psalm is and he can say some parts with me. Then we talked about King David. Manuel looked at the book and sat very still.

"Did the prophets really know that Jesus was coming?"

"Yes, they knew because God had promised a redeemer to mankind when he locked them out of paradise."

"What is a redeemer?" Peter wants to know.

"It's like letting someone go when you play cops and robbers."

"That is a very good explanation, Andrew! After Adam and Eve sinned, heaven was closed and all the people like Noah, Abraham, Moses, David . . ."

"Daniel," says a small voice which belongs to Manuel. He has no idea of what we are discussing but the name David suggests "Daniel" to him. We all laugh, but we are proud of him.

"When these people died, they could not go into paradise. They had to wait in a place of the dead until the redeemer came for them to lead them to heaven."

"Is that purgatory, Mommy?"

"They called it limbo although I don't think this is a very good name for it."

"But it wasn't heaven. And it is sad for the dead somewhere else," says Andrew.

"But we always sing in Advent: 'O Saviour, rend the heavens,' or 'Lift up your gates.' Adam and Eve were disobedient to God and he had to send them out of paradise. He also put an angel at its entrance. The heavens were closed. But God made them a promise: 'The redeemer will come and will open the gates of heaven again.' How long the Jews had to wait and how they cried out: 'Come, Saviour, come.' And Jesus, the Son of the Father, the Son of God, came. He who had been with the Father from all eternity came to people at Christmas. Now we know that Jesus has come."

"And that he died," says Andrew.

"And that heaven is open again and that Jesus went back to heaven after his death and is with the Father. Do you know now why the birth of Jesus is something to be happy about?"

After that we recited the creed. The three Advent candles were burning. When we came to the "descended into hell," Andrew kept very still and said breathlessly,

"Did he get all of them, —Moses, David, and everyone?"

"Yes, he brought them to heaven to God. He ascended into heaven; on the third day he rose again from the dead . . ."

"But the Christ Child will be coming soon," says Peter, content now with serious matters. How happy they became over the feast! They knew that I would be looking after the gifts for them. "But the Christ Child decides who receives the gifts." That is indeed not far from the truth. We parents decide, but God is the one who has placed us by the side of our children.

Helen is visiting because she wants to help me out a bit. In the evening when the boys had gone out she observed somewhat thoughtfully, "But they have no idea of what they are saying when they pray."

"No, they don't. At least the smallest ones don't. But it is my experience that they ought to learn a few prayers like the Our Father, the Hail Mary, the Creed, and the Confiteor gradually. It need not be done all at once. . . . But, for example, a child can stand the Our Father said slowly, the Hail Mary repeated like a greeting, the advertence to the doings of the day, and a small original prayer. A child loves ritual. It loves actions which can be repeated regularly. Regularity means security, safety, and happiness to a child.

Manuel knows that he is allowed into my room for ten minutes every day after breakfast.

I have a little table and chair for just that purpose. He sits down and starts looking at a book which is not too lovely but does contain pictures by Rembrandt. What goes through his mind? He always picks out the same pictures and looks at them a long time. I say casually, "That is Isaac. That is Ganymede. That is Absalom who is crying."

He looks at one of the pictures. A man is lying on a stretcher and men are standing all around him. One of them is teaching. Then Manuel says all of a sudden, "Dead. Dead man." How does he know that?

Ever since that day this picture is daily contemplated and this has become a ritual with him. It does not seem to disturb him that I may be tidying the room or sewing on something. At the last picture he shuts the book closed and returns it to its place. Then he goes into the garden to play. But tomorrow he will find the book in the same place and the same ritual will be gone through again. A child is not always looking for something new as adults imagine. A child attaches himself to an old acquaintance and only then does it add what is new, more or less according to his stage of development. It is the same with prayer and with stories from the Bible. A child's joy in something he knows is just as great every time. His enthusiasm in being able to speak words he already knows is of utmost importance. For this reason children can be taught real prayers without any worry. A real Our Father is sometimes better for a child than a too-childish prayer. An all-too-childish prayer, I believe, is not worth the recommending.

Did Jesus have friends?

Christmas. The lowliness of God. The nativity story according to the Gospel. Andrew and the distribution of gifts. The positive power of a child's imagination and the notion of truth. Participation of grown-ups in the thought processes of the child. Grown-ups and children. Praise in the psalms. St. Stephen. The hidden life of Jesus. John the apostle and the Mother of God at the cross. Mary's obedience. Saying yes. St. Therese of Lisieux. Personal relation to the saints. St. Teresa of Avila.

THIS evening when the children are asleep, we are going to set up the tree. There will be a place for you, too, Isabel, so that tomorrow's events will go along without mishap. This year I made my Christmas packages for all the godchildren, relatives, the needy, and friends in November. I never succeeded in doing this before. Now we can celebrate Advent and the Christmas time in peace, with a greater sense of the mystery and with greater joy because there will be no hustling and bustling. This time I had much more time for the children, their presents, their surprises, and their questions.

Our parish priest came to the house to bless Isabel. The baptism will take place on December 28th and Andrew and Peter will assist the priest. They were all excited when they heard about it. "With a real red cassock? Isabel can never be an altar boy. She is a girl and only boys can be altar boys!"

"She can work in the church," commented good little Peter reassuringly. She can light the candles and put them out. And she can clean the church!"

In the meantime the baptismal robe and little undergarment were prepared. I wonder how many generations in the family have already worn it, I mused, as I hung the long white gown on a hanger.

The temperature has dropped. The sky is bright with stars and the air is crisp from the cold. We shall have to dress you very warmly, my darling Isabel.

Christmas was just wonderful with the new baby. First we sang songs while father held the baby. Andrew went through the Christmas story very beautifully, slowly and without mistake. Peter came in at the end with "Fear not." And he whispered, "I say it right, Mommy," and Manuel closed with "Amen."

"And she brought forth her first-born son, and wrapped him in swaddling clothes, and laid him in a manger, because there was no room for them in the inn." —Who can ever estimate how much suffering, weariness, anxiety, trust, poverty, joy, love, renunciation, humility, and modesty lies concealed in this simple narrative? I understand better with each new birth and I have told this to the children, too. We shudder at the sweetish descriptions of the birth of Jesus. We are appalled by the falseness of this arrival, where the stable is a drawing room with friendly domestic animals—ox and ass—where need and poverty are pushed out and nothing remains of the reality. The children show concern for Mary's painful journey to Bethlehem. They know how it was with me before Isabel was born. They see how solicitous Joseph is, how attentive and kind he is to Mary. They sense how lonely these two people must have been in the stable and they sympathetically contemplate the poorest of all births. One should not deviate from the words of the sacred text, and only afterwards should explanation follow. Here is the redeemer of the world, the Son of God, this little child before whom shepherds and kings bend the knee, who took it upon himself to become man in order to reconcile God and man.

Father went to midnight Mass without me and the children. They are too small, but Andrew might be able to go next year. He wants to so much. The bells have already rung. The sky is overcast and there is a little snow on the ground. Once in a while moonbeams break through the snow clouds. I had to give up going to church for a while because it is still too strenuous for me. By the time of the baptism I hope to be all right.

Today was quiet and peaceful. In the morning the older children went to Mass with Rose. After this they went tobogganing with the new sled. In the afternoon about five o'clock we lit the candles on the Christmas tree. Andrew asked me to fix everything just the way it was last evening at the gift-giving. I even had to ring the Christmas bell because he wanted to recite the Christmas story. We sang many songs. There are such lovely ones. . . . I sang to them from the Christmas oratorio. Andrew surprised us all by looking at the presents as if he had never seen them before. He showed us everything. The lion which he had already taken to bed with him was rediscovered and held out to me triumphantly. My friend Barbara was present and she whispered to me with not a little anxiety, "Aren't you worried about this make-believe? He's deceiving himself and he knows it. If you let this game continue, aren't you fostering a tendency to untruth?" I asked her to wait and to let things take their natural course. When the children were called in to take their bath Andrew passed by me, remained standing, and said quietly, "It was just as pretty as yesterday, yesterday and today. Know what, Mommy? I'm just so happy about everything!"

I believe that this ability to be happy all over again, this power of the imagination, this capacity to enter into things, is a gift which we should take care of and develop. It can be a grace.

I kept thinking of Barbara for a long time. Truth! To instill this into a child demands the greatest caution, the greatest empathy. A child has a much greater affinity for the supernatural than adults have. Children are still living in a sort of paradise where they enjoy a direct communication with God and his angels. Let us take care not to do harm to this blessing. It is for us to learn from them.

We have no idea how deeply thoughtless or hasty words can hurt a child. We should never tire of listening to a child when he has something to tell us even if what he has to say is poorly formulated. I have always been grateful when one of my children has initiated me into his way of thinking, and I have awakened sometimes in the night only to be tortured by the thought that I had not had enough patience that day with Andrew, or Peter, or Manuel, or with some other child. I had listened to only half of what the child wanted to say and I had left him lonely. I had not helped him. The memory of a premature judgment about some childish problem has come back to startle me, and I feel the millstone which belongs around my neck if I have scandalized one of these little ones. However, one should not take a too tragic view of all this, but there should be profit from an experience of this kind to do better the next time. One should always act with moderation, trying not to come too close to a child's world by making a forced entrance into this mysterious land lest the child be stifled or crushed.

In the evening we read this beautiful psalm:

> Praise the Lord from the heavens,
>   praise him in the heights;
> Praise him, all you his angels,
>   praise him, all you his hosts.

> Praise him, sun and moon;
>   praise him, all you shining stars.
> Praise him, you highest heavens,
>   and you waters above the heavens.
> Let them praise the name of the Lord,
>   for he commanded and they were created;

He established them forever and ever;
    he gave them a duty which shall not pass away.

Praise the Lord from the earth,
    you sea monsters and all depths;
Fire and hail, snow and mist,
    storm winds that fulfill his word;
You mountains and all you hills,
    you fruit trees and all you cedars;
You wild beasts and all tame animals,
    you creeping things and you winged fowl.

Let the kings of the earth and all peoples,
    the princes and all the judges of the earth,
Young men too, and maidens,
    old men and boys,
Praise the name of the Lord,
    for his name alone is exalted. . . .

The whole story of Noah's ark was just too much for Peter, who called out at the end of the story, "I praise the Lord. The fir tree, my balls, my animals, my books, and Isabel, all, —they all praise the Lord!" Children are generally sensitive to praise. It is good for them to learn to praise God in psalm when they are growing up.

Today is the feast of St. Stephen, the first martyr, and tomorrow is the feast of St. John. I have read to the children from the Scriptures. "It is terrible to throw stones," said Andrew indignantly. "I am a martyr," said Peter. "Rudy threw stones at me yesterday." I explained to my martyr about Stephen's courage when he spoke to the members of the synagogue.

"He had courage because he was full of the Holy Spirit who gives strength to do impossible things and to die for Jesus."

"Wasn't he afraid?"

"No, he saw the heavens open suddenly and the Son of Man, Jesus, was sitting at the right hand of God."

"Because he had already risen?"

"Yes, and he and God the Father and the Holy Spirit are one."

"When we know that we have Jesus we can do everything, can't we, Mommy?"

"But just the same, I would have been a little afraid," said Peter, "but I know that Jesus is here."

"And did St. John die too?"

"Yes, but he was not a martyr."

"He wore a camel skin," said Peter.

"No, darling Peter, my martyr. We are not talking about John the Baptist. We are talking about the apostle John. You know, the one whom Jesus loved so much, the one who was his friend."

"Did Jesus have friends?" Andrew is somewhat amazed.

"Of course he did. Jesus was human. He was just like us."

"Could he eat?" asks Peter.

"Why certainly! He went to a wedding, for example. He and his mother had received an invitation."

"A real invitation?" The two of them looked at me with unbelief in their eyes.

"Yes, they had been asked to come because there was going to be a marriage feast. Get the picture Bible. I'll show you the picture of the wedding feast at Cana."

"What is in the great big jars?" Peter was referring to the jars filled with water.

"Water. The water had to be drawn from the well."

"Had John been invited too?" Andrew tossed in. He always liked to hear one story after the other.

"John was probably there, too, although the Bible doesn't say so exactly. But wait! I'll show you a picture of John with Jesus. Grandfather always had this picture on his writing desk."

"He's sleeping!"

"Yes, he's sleeping. He's sitting very close to Jesus, and because he's so tired, he leans his head on Jesus and Jesus remains quiet in order not to disturb his sleeping friend. He even holds him up just as if John were a child, a tired little child. Get the picture Bible again. See, here is Jesus on the cross. His mother and John are both standing there. Jesus is going to die and although he can hardly talk any longer, he looks at his mother and John and he says to John, 'My mother is your mother now.' Then he says to his mother, 'Mother, John will be your son now.' He could have said, 'Mother, Andrew is your son now. Soon I shall be here no longer. I shall be in heaven with my Father and my mother whom I love will not be alone. John will comfort her and she will comfort him. He will take her home with him so that she will not have to go back to an empty house.' Jesus is thinking about everything when he says to John, 'John, my mother is now your mother.'"

"And was he really her son?"

"Oh yes, he was. And Mary became his mother. She was so obedient in everything. The last words of her son were very holy to her."

"But they were not really Jesus' last words because he rose again."

47

"This was one of the last things he said before he died. Jesus said to his mother, 'John is your child and with him take all people on earth as your children.' So, she is our mother, our blessed mother. Mary is the queen of all saints. She always said yes. 'Yes, God. Yes, I obey. Yes, I am a handmaid of the Lord.' She was able to say yes because she loved God above all things."

"But St. Stephen loved God, too, more than anything else," says Andrew "or else he would not have died for Jesus."

"The saints have always believed, 'God may do with us what he wants. He knows best. Nothing can happen to us. We shall go to God when we die.' The saints pray for us and they help us. They are very close to God and they know how to ask for what we need."

"Peter!" "Yes, Lord." "Stop quarreling." "Yes, Lord!" "Andrew, be patient because you love me." "Yes, Lord!"

"If we say that, does it mean that we are a little bit holy?" asks Peter. "That's the way to holiness. The little St. Therese always said yes. But nobody noticed that she was saying yes. Nobody praised her. Nobody encouraged her. She performed a thousand small humble services and loving deeds for those around her. She didn't answer with unkind words. She accepted the indifference of others. 'Yes, Lord, for you.' She is a great saint, as great as the saint for whom she was named, the great St. Teresa of Avila whom I love so much."

"You have a picture of her on your writing desk!"

"If I am writing and happen to look up I see her picture and I am filled with love for her ardent soul, her great heart, her understanding, and her humility."

"Do you know her that well, Mommy?"

"I have read a great deal about her, much of which she wrote herself. So, I know her well. That is why your little sister is called Isabel Teresa. I want to bring you together with many saints. You are the friends of Jesus and they were, too. This is how you are related. Your father and I have a personal reason for each of your names."

Why does she cry so much
if she doesn't have any sins?

Private baptism. Role of the godparents. The godmother and
the mother. The actual relation of parent to parent. Security of
the child. Isabel is nursed. The proper approach to questions per-
taining to life. A healthy curiosity. The unanswered questions
of the child. The "embarrassment" of parents. The child asks
about the mysteries of life. A false discretion. When to explain.
The young mother of God and the angel. How can this be? The
plan of God. Marriage is a sacrament. Isabel's baptism. The soul
and free will. The conscience. Truth. Fear of punishment. Self-
punishment. What does the soul say? The soul of Adam and Eve
before the first sin. Jesus, the redeemer. Reflections after the bap-
tism. Isabel, you are my child. My house is your house. The bap-
tismal candle. Take care of your light.

THE nurse came to ask if Isabel should be baptized in the
hospital. The Church prefers to have a child baptized without
delay because it could die without baptism. Manuel was baptized privately. His little flame of life was flickering low. He
came into the world hardly breathing, lying white and motion-
less, so I baptized him immediately. I sent for holy water although I could have used other water in case of emergency and

I said: "Manuel, I baptize you in the name of the Father and of the Son and of the Holy Spirit." Manuel remained a long time more ready for heaven than for earth.

In Isabel's case I wanted to wait until I got home because I wanted to take part in the celebration just as much as the godparents did. Mamina, our friend, will be able to come, and so will John.

We ourselves have many godchildren for whom we have promised to see to it that they become and remain good Christians.

Andrew and Peter have their Mamina. How important her role is! How important that along with their own mother the children respect someone they can love and in whose presence they feel secure and confident. Mamina really lives up to her obligation. Every year since we have been married she has spent a few weeks with us and these days belonged first to Andrew and Peter but later also to Manuel. She has something in her which can never be lost to the children. She has ardor, faith, a sense of honor, respect and magnanimity. They received their picture Bible from her. What little mother says goes. They instinctively feel her piety, her faith, her vigor, vitality and cleverness. Our children's relation to her is extraordinarily important and a great help to me.

Children naturally love father and mother, but not all parents advert to the fact that children should not be tied too much to them. Many times it is a great sacrifice not to help a child. Sometimes we must deny our help which would make him dependent and establish a false relation of child to parent. This goes especially for the boys in the family who have an ambivalent relation to their mother. Almost every boy has wanted to marry his mother. Almost every little girl has wanted to marry her father. How flattering this little lover is for a mother. But she must bring her child very early to an understanding of the unreality of such a situation. It can be best achieved by the child's appreciation of the living relation between parents. The mother-child relation grows best in this soil.

I shall never forget the declaration of my three-year-old Andrew: "Papa, I love you now just as much as I love Mommy!" That was a long way for him and for me, —this oldest child of mine from whom I received most of my experience, whom I have known and loved the longest. It is important for a child to be aware of the living relation which exists between the parents. In it they feel safe and secure.

Who has not been acquainted with a child's horror when he sees nervous or overworked parents losing patience with each other or resorting to deathlike coldness instead of appealing to some solution of the difficulty? Such a child is not only dismissed from his paradise, but he also loses the precious help he needs to master his own life.

The children's father sat a long time by me and Isabel in spite of all the work he had to do. "It is reassuring here, my darling." With that Peter stormed in without even knocking. He stood there puzzled and embarrassed, went back out, knocked at the door, came in again and said, "I didn't know you loved each other!"

"We've always loved each other . . ."

"I mean when Papa sits near you . . ."

Later the three boys were sitting by me. Isabel was sleeping in her crib, fragile and yet so full of energy. They have accepted you into their circle, all three, and I have to restrain their demonstrations of love. This morning Manuel wanted to smother you under a toy when Peter decided picture books were better. I saved you in the nick of time. Each day one of the boys is allowed to help me when you have your bath. It is almost a religious rite. Then the "help" arranges my bed and asks very casually, "Which side?" They think it is tremendously important that Isabel be comfortable when she is being nursed and they are very anxious that she get enough.

A young woman, a neighbor of mine, visited me yesterday morning as I was nursing Isabel. Manuel was sitting by my bed on a little chair playing with blocks at a table.

"Do you allow the children to watch?" she asked, a little shocked.

"Yes, why?"

"Aren't you afraid that they might entertain some foolish notions?"

"That is the last thing I am thinking of!" But I knew that I would have to be patient, taking trouble to give an answer.

"Foolish notions? I believe that this practical and gradual way of instructing my children will only come to good. Their wanting to know is not curiosity but something quite natural. This is one way of satisfying a healthy inquisitiveness. And isn't it better that the information should come from me rather than from perhaps a school chum? The mystery of life retains its greatness, and oppressive, mysterious dissembling is avoided."

"My son doesn't have the slightest thoughts about such matters!"

"How old is he now?"

"Seven!"

"Don't you think that he might be thinking sooner than you want him to?" She blushed and answered very quickly, "He has never said a word but this morning he came very early into our bedroom and merely said, 'I just wanted to see what you are doing' —and, oh, I can't tell you. . . ."

"Why not? We are both grown-ups, and except for the things which only concern you and your husband, why shouldn't we speak about everything? How are you going to confront your child later if you are embarrassed in front of me?" She calmed herself a bit. "The day before yesterday I found a terribly indecent drawing which my son had made."

Once again she was very embarrassed. "This is what my boy has drawn!"

"But didn't you just finish telling me he has never given such matters a thought?"

"Oh, I'm so disturbed. I haven't even told my husband. He would pulverize the boy!"

"I think, dear Mrs. B., that both you and your husband are to blame for the drawing."

She was very horrified. "We? We do so much for the child's protection. . . ."

"Yes," I interrupted, "and deprive him of everything which the Church demands of you."

She stared at me unbelievingly.

"Yes, the Church! Do you remember the talk I was asked to give by the Church last year? No, you were sick at the time. The mind of the Church in this matter is very clear: an early explanation by the parents, at the very latest by the seventh year and precisely because of the danger to which a child is exposed. Look at the Mother of God. When the angel Gabriel came to her and announced that she would bear a son, what kind of an answer did she immediately give?"

The woman stammered: "Behold the handmaid of the Lord . . ."

"No, Mrs. B. First she said: 'How can this be done since I know no man!' And how old was Mary? Fourteen or fifteen, not any more. Do you think that knowledge of the mysteries of life did any harm to the purity of the Mother of God? This knowledge will do just as little harm to your child. He will only be saved by it. The picture he made is just a sign of his torment. You are dragging the mysteries of God and his creation in the dirt when you call them 'such matters.' These matters are the work of a loving God. This is the way we should accept them and esteem them. Don't you think so? And why don't you want to talk the matter over with your husband? In the final analysis, hasn't he been joined to you in the sacrament of matrimony in the creation of your child? And this happened not secretly in sin and fear but, on the contrary, with joy in the holy state of marriage. You belong to him! Married people should be one flesh and one heart and mind. You must help your child and just as soon as possible. Naturally, it will be harder for you than if you had let that knowledge grow gradually. Does Martin know that you are expecting a new baby?"

"No, I thought he hadn't noticed it yet!"

"But he should notice it and he should be happy about it. He ought to be learning to take consideration of his mother. He ought to be aware of the relation between you and your husband."

"You are probably right," sighed the poor woman as she departed somewhat perturbed. She wanted to come back at the end of the week. That gave me much to think about. How will these parents conduct themselves when their son reaches puberty if they are so helpless now?

On the 28th of December the baby was baptized. It was overwhelming. We drove to the church at five o'clock in the afternoon. It was getting dark. The bells were ringing. The church was dark and empty. We waited for our pastor at the back of the church, at the door. Andrew and Peter had already been brought to the sacristy a half-hour earlier in order to vest for the ceremony. I gave Mamina the baby. Grandmother was standing near me and father held my arm. At the side of Mamina stood the lanky John happy and touched in a coat which was much too thin. Finally the sacristy door opened gradually and Andrew and Peter appeared very slowly in white starched surplices, behind them our parish priest and the wife of the sacristan. Andrew held the baptismal candle which was blessed and Peter held the white robe, symbol of purity. They came towards us slowly and devoutly, conscious of their dignity, Peter full of business and Andrew a dreamy ecstatic angel.

It was still and beautiful. Isabel was very good and did not cry. The dark church was decorated for Christmas and it was filled with the scent of pine and incense. How meaningful it all of a sudden seemed to me: "I have called you by name." I was so excited that I could not recite the creed. After the ceremony we went home. The baby was nursed and we sat down to an early supper at which only the parents, grandparents, and godparents were present.

The three boys appeared after their bath and they were radiant with joy. We prayed at the crib of the newly baptized Isabel. Thereupon Andrew and Peter became alive with questions.

.

"Everyone has a soul and something else. But I can't remember now. . . ."

"A soul and free will. Adam could decide whether he wanted to obey or not. You can decide whether you want to take a glass of jelly secretly in the garden room or whether you will tell me you would like some jelly. Only you can say to your voice, 'Say yes, say no.'"

"But sometimes you say it!"

"I?"

"Yes, you in me. Once in Summer I heard you say in me, 'Don't go to the water barrel. You could fall in and drown. Don't go.' I held my feet with my hands so that they would not run to it. Then I drew a line in front of the barrel so that I could not go farther. That was just because you were scolding inside me!"

"This voice was your conscience. Everybody has such a voice which advises, 'That is good. That is not good. That is danger-

57

ous. Don't do it. It is forbidden.' But did you obey your voice?"

"Yes. I was afraid. But, Mommy, I went later to the water barrel!"

"And when I asked you, did you tell me the truth?"

"No, because I was afraid!"

I remember. He told me solemnly that he had not been near the water cistern and I had praised him. A half-hour later he came to me with a bleeding knee but he was not crying.

He had fallen somewhere near the barrel. He seemed to be having some pain, but he looked at the wound indifferently and seemed uninterested in my tending it. "It is a punishment, I think."

"A punishment? What for?"

"For things that I have done which were naughty, but before, when I was small . . ."

He had punished himself. One must recognize this form of expiation and learn to hold back one's own preachments.

"You told us that people have a soul and that animals don't. Does Isabel have a soul? She can't even talk."

"But she had a soul from the very beginning just like everybody else."

"What is a soul?" Peter wanted to know.

"When somebody loves," answers Andrew very simply.

"And when one thinks," adds Peter, shedding light on the matter.

"The life in people which cannot be seen, like thinking and loving."

"And when someone wants something or doesn't want it," I

continue. "The will is also a power of the soul. 'I don't want to obey now,' you say sometimes. 'I've decided to do something else and not what Mommy wants.'"

"Aw," says Peter disillusioned, "I meant that the soul is always good."

"Adam and Eve had souls which were perfectly good and pure, and their souls were like God who is a spirit. We can't see him. He can be seen only with the soul. There isn't too much to say. It is a mystery which is too great.

"When Adam and Eve did not obey God their souls became darkened and they could not recognize God any more. He went as far away from them as he had come near them in the Garden of Paradise. No one was allowed into heaven after this.

"Only after the redeemer Jesus had come did heaven open up. But our hearts became darkened, too. When your face is not clean, and I can hardly recognize you, I wash it and then I look again into your dear face, Peter. That is what God does at baptism. He washes Isabel's heart clean from the sin of Adam. Baptismal water purifies, sanctifies; without water our flowers would die. When you pour water on them they come back to life and live again. So it is with baptismal water. We live again. The darkened heart becomes bright and light again."

"But why does she shriek all the time if she doesn't have any sin?"

"Because we are living on earth and no longer in paradise."

"Too bad! We could have gone around very happy with no clothes on and you would not have had to do the wash."

"And Miss Meyer would also have come to the office naked," says Peter.

"I couldn't even imagine such a thing," Andrew adds.

"No one could imagine such a thing because we don't live in paradise," I try to explain. "But God wants to live in us. He wants to be in people. He wants to have them all and they are supposed to be his children. God says, 'Isabel, you are my child. You know me now. You hear my voice. You can hear me when I call now. I love you, my child.'"

"God has lots of children!"

"Yes, he has, and still, when we talk with God we are his only child and he is our only father."

"Why couldn't Isabel go to church right away?"

"Because she was not baptized yet, because the church was not her house yet. But now the church is her house just as it is yours. You will go to communion in this house. You will go to confession in it and perhaps you will even marry in this church. You will be buried in this church, perhaps. . . ."

"No, not in it, in the cemetery."

"Yes, of course, but the funeral Mass is celebrated in the church. And just think how often we go to Mass in this church!"

Yesterday Isabel went there to be baptized, —in this house of God.

"Isabel Teresa, I baptize you in the name of the Father, and of the Son, and of the Holy Spirit," said our pastor, and he poured water on Isabel's head. She became a child of God immediately and a sister of Jesus. . . ."

"What about the Holy Spirit?"

"He is in her!"

"What happened to the candle, Mommy? Can we burn it at night in the children's room?"

"No, only on feast days in the church. Remember what the pastor said to Isabel:

" 'Receive this burning light and cherish the grace of baptism. Keep the commandments of God. When the Lord comes with all the saints of heaven, you can come to him and enter into paradise forever.'

"Jesus says, 'I am the light of the world.' And Isabel stands in this light. Take care of your light. Don't let it go out. Don't let it grow dim. Shield it from bad winds, from evil hands, who will want to take your light away. . . .'

"That is the devil!"

"Yes, that is he because he hates the beautiful light."

"The white baptismal robe also shows how white, how pure the soul should be. God looks at his child. He likes to look at the soul of a little child. He says to Isabel, 'How like my Son you are, my Son Jesus Christ. How well I can see you now in this beautiful light."

I must never forget this lovely psalm:

O Lord, let the light of your countenance shine upon us!
You put gladness into my heart,
more than when grain and wine abound.

61

Why didn't my angel
take care of me?

*You lied. False accusations. An extorted confession. God will pun-
ish you. A wrong concept of God. The misguided child. The
guardian angel. The angels before the creation of the world.
Lucifer. Michael. Why the Old Testament? Why not only the
New Testament? Adam after his sin. The Old Testament. Life
without grace. Jesus, the redeemer. Jesus, the reconciler with
God. The Jews waiting for the redeemer. Customs of the Jews.
Their faith. Their life with our God before Jesus came. The
Old Testament, no fairy tale. Leading to Jesus.*

SOMETHING bad happened today. Our nursemaid accused Peter
of lying.

She doesn't like him and that's very clear. She likes only
babies. She asked him if he had broken the pot in the kitchen.

"No." And Peter had run off again. She called him back and
told him that he had certainly done it. He had been in the
kitchen.

"You're lying," she said sternly to Peter. He looked at her
devoid of understanding.

"You broke the pot. What will God say? He will certainly
punish you."

"Well, maybe I did break it a little," said poor Peter. The nurse maid was triumphant.

"You've lied. God doesn't like liars!"

I knew nothing of the whole affair. I knew only that Peter seemed to be downcast about something when he came to me in the afternoon after his nap. I had been looking for a pen which the children seem to like very much, and while I was conducting my search I asked casually, "Would you know what happened to my pen?"

"No," answered Peter worriedly, "no, I really don't know. Did I lie now?"

"What do you mean?" I stopped now to listen and noticed the worried look in his face. "What do you mean *lied*? Peter, what is wrong?" "I didn't break the pot," he swallowed. "I don't know where the pen is."

Just at this point Mrs. Tanner knocked. Mrs. Tanner helped me in the house sometimes and now she came with her son who was somewhat younger than Peter. She wanted to say goodbye.

"Come," she said to the child, "tell Mrs. Becker what you did!"

In short, the child had broken the pot. But Peter was inconsolable and in this way I found out the whole story. Now, the nursemaid is staying another week. . . . Peter has been confronted by an evil world.

Isabel, when you have your own child, beware of an exaggerated love of truth. That doesn't mean that Peter will never lie in his life. No, but a lightly tossed off "You are lying" could distort one's natural sense of the truth. Now his paradise has collapsed and he is insecure. Up to this time he has always answered yes or no calmly and truthfully, without fear and without threat.

How foolish and wrong it is to use God as a threat. The nursemaid could have said to him, "God knows everything. He sees everything." But she should not have demeaned God to an object of threat.

It took a long time to reassure Peter. He often wanted to know if he had lied. But he also asked, "Tell me, Mommy, why didn't my angel take care of me?"

"But he did take care of you!"

"No, not quite. I'm still very sad, because I didn't do it."

"But, Peter, I know what happened. You know and your angel knows. Don't be sad."

"Tell me, Mommy, Andrew wants to know. Does Isabel already have an angel?"

"Yes, she does, a great big beautiful angel. Everybody has such a servant of God."

"Servant?"

"Yes, you know that in the beginning before the world was created God had only angels with him. They served him. Angels, spirits, cannot be seen. When they come with a message from God, Andrew, people are frightened. The Mother of God was frightened when Gabriel came to her and so were the shepherds. Angels take on a body like ours, but the eternity out of which they come shines in their eyes. That is what makes people like us tremble. Among these angels, these wonderful beings, there was one who was particularly beautiful. His name was Lucifer and God loved him very much. But he was proud, so proud that he thought he could be like God. And then the archangel Michael came and with a very strong voice he cried out, 'Who is like God?' The name Michael means 'Who is like God?' His voice was terrible. And the angels on Michael's side began to fight with the angels on Lucifer's side. It was a battle which was a matter of life and death. Michael, the beautiful angel, won. But the disobedient angels were plunged into the depths from which they could never come back to God again. Later, everyone who was born into the world received an angel who was supposed to guide him. And whether we want it or not, he is always near us because God has sent him and he obeys God.

"So Isabel has an angel guardian too. The angel stays with Isabel and does what God wants him to do. Most people think that only children have an angel. We all have one. Sometimes we forget this."

Today Barbara wrote, "Why do you talk to the children so much about the Old Testament? Aren't the good tidings and the teachings of Jesus of more importance for them?"

"My dear Barbara, it seems important to me that our children should become acquainted with the story of their forefathers of their faith. They should know about their relation to the great Yahweh. They should learn about the story of their salvation.

" 'Why do they always talk about salvation, Mommy?' asks Manuel. And Andrew gave him a very good answer. 'If you're caught when you're playing cops and robbers, you wait patiently and just wish and wish for someone to free you so that you can run around again. You want to get out of your prison.' It's just the same with Jesus. He lets us out of prison. But if this captivity has no meaning for children, the coming of Jesus will also have no meaning. And what you would like to communicate to the children will be lost, dear Barbara. I know that I'm not saying anything new but just let me go over it once again. —Adam did not listen to God. He disobeyed him and as a consequence he experienced the difference between what was good and what was not good and above all he became acquainted with death. Up to this time Adam had lived in perfect unity with God in paradise. God had dealt with him. God had thought with him. All of a sudden Adam refused to do what God wanted. He wanted to know what God knows. He was proud, too. But what he succeeded in knowing was terrible. He hid from God. He was no longer on good terms with him. He stood alone. He and Eve became fearful. They had a feeling which they had never had before. They were ashamed of their nakedness, of their having yielded. They became afraid. They had slipped away from the grace of God. God was angry with them and he closed the door of his companionship. And now Adam's troubles on earth began, —not only his troubles but also the troubles of his children and his children's children.

"But in all of the frightfulness of the situation God promised Adam a Saviour who would one day redeem him, who would finally end the separation of God and man, who would reunite them and reconcile them. There is only one who could do that and he was the Son of God, God himself as man.[1] He would

---

[1] *For Jesus was with the Father from eternity.*

come as man from the race of the Jews. That is what I told Manuel.

"Don't you think it is a rewarding experience, Barbara, to give the children an idea of the way which the Jews travelled for thousands of years while they were waiting for the redeemer? Don't you think they ought to know about the many great people who besought God to have mercy on them? And shouldn't they be aware of the humiliation they suffered and of the hope they carried with them? Isn't this the way to make their redemption have more meaning for them, obliging them to greater gratitude? Their customs and ceremonies, their alliance with God, and the commandments which gave direction to their lives up to the birth of Christ continue to this day. I often think that we live like the unredeemed people of that time with one difference, —we cry wearily for redemption. Redemption has already come to us but we do not accept it. 'My yoke is sweet.' What meaning can the paschal meal have for the children, that meal which Jesus wanted to hold for the last time with his apostles, if they don't know about the exodus from Egypt, the oppression in Egypt, or if they don't know who Moses was who received the commandments according to which we live? What was the manna, the bread from heaven? How was the notion of the Eucharist received? 'Give me of this water that I may never thirst again!' asked the Samaritan woman at the well of Jacob. Jacob, the father of the twelve tribes of Israel among whom was Judah—who stands in the genealogy of Jesus and from whom Joseph of the house of David the husband of Mary descended—had watered his herds at this well.

"Children should know about the Old Testament not only because it is the story of the Jews, God's chosen people, but because they ought to know how much God has done for us all from the very beginning. Children should be taught to appreciate the fact of God's mercy on erring mankind and of his help in restoring the bond between God and man. It seems to me that the Old Testament can be compared to the situation of men who are sailing around astray on a ship who, after terrible danger, endless hopelessness, disappointments, and ruinous despair, finally renew their hope, trust again, summon their strength, and find their way back to the harbor. It seems to me that the prayer, 'Thy kingdom come,' means that and nothing else. Jesus is that kingdom of God which we are building up with all our strength until the coming of Christ again.

"Therefore I try to acquaint my children with everything in which God had a hand. It ought to make a great impression on them and it does in fact. But it depends on me whether the children receive this narration as a fairy tale or whether they stand in awe of it before this great holy God, the Father of Jesus Christ. I want so much to convince you. Think about this tomorrow at Mass. I will go to the altar of God."

Where is Abraham waiting?

Sickness and death. Do I have to die? Prayer in need. Hope and despair. The rich glutton and the poor Lazarus. Why didn't Lazarus go to heaven? A closed heaven. Only the death of Jesus can redeem mankind. Where is Abraham waiting? The pains of hell. Eternal abandonment. Moses and the commandments. Our commandments. What is a prophet? Even when people see the miracles of God they do not believe. The youth of Nain. Life and death. What is decomposition? Loving the dead. Jesus is stronger than death. Jesus arouses the young man. Elijah, the prophet, also restores life. "I say to you, arise." Lord, God of Sabaoth, help me to restore life to this child. A Jewish burial. Why did Jairus call Jesus? "Little maiden, I say to you, arise." The woman who was sick for twelve years meets Jesus. If I could only touch the hem of his garment. Power has gone out from me. The cure. Conscience and the courage to tell the truth.

ANDREW was very sick. We did not know exactly what it was and even the doctor was not sure. When acute appendicitis developed, even a ruptured appendix, the doctor ordered the immediate transfer of Andrew to the hospital. Andrew lay very still, looking small and pale. His hands were hot and he kept looking at the window.

"My darling, we have to go to the hospital immediately. You have to have an operation."

Andrew was frightened but he controlled himself and said, "Do I have to go right away?"

"Right away. We have no time to lose."

"Do I have to die, Mommy?" He asked this question calmly but it made me tremble.

"Mommy, do I have to die? Tell me. I still have so many things to think about. . . ."

"What things?"

"About God. . . ."

I carried him to the car. What one can do when one has to! Outdoors the thermometer showed below zero. The car didn't start at once. The ride was tiring and I trembled with agonizing fear.

"Don't be worried, Mommy," came the tired voice again. "I'm not going to die."

Then he became quiet; too quiet. I looked back anxiously and drove on.

As he lay on the stretcher in the hospital he said, "I've said all my prayers. You don't have to worry. Just stay with me." His small hand held on to mine and his eyes searched my own. He even smiled.

"You must have confidence," I said as calmly as possible. "Everything is going to be all right."

"Yes," answered Andrew. "Make the sign of the cross on me and I shall do the same to you."

He traced a small cross on my forehead.

"Recite the psalm for me: 'And even though I walk in the valley of darkness . . .'" That was a hard test. My voice failed but at the same time I calmed down. I was allowed to stay with him until the medication began to take effect. His small hand became limp and then I had to leave the operating room.

"You will have him back in half an hour," said the doctor.

O God, do not take him from me. O God, if it is your will take him. Forgive me my first prayer. Leave me my child. Let me accept your will in his regard.

Even though I walk in the valley of darkness . . . O Mother of God, you surely know how I feel. Reassure me. Help me. Take care of him. Pray for us, O Mother of Jesus!

I waited one hour and three quarters. As the child was carried by me on a stretcher, a nurse who did not notice me said, "I wonder if he'll come out of it?"

"Sh!" said the other and she pointed to me. A few hours later Andrew awakened.

"Mommy, thank God," he said, and succumbed to an attack of nausea. Later I sat by his bed listening to his breathing. It was almost dark in the room. Did I still hear him? O my God, after so much renewed hope is he going to slip away from me now without a sound?

"Mommy, hold me, you are so far away. . . ." He took my hand and fell into a deep quiet sleep already on the road to recovery.

"Right? People have to keep hurrying in life, or else . . ."

"Or else what?"

71

"Or else people would die and then there would be no more time and the people would have to wait, Mommy. We would have to wait a long time. . . . You read to us that one never knows when the bridegroom is coming and so we should always be ready."

"What should we have ready, Andrew?"

"Our heart, and what we think. Then when Jesus comes no one would be surprised or afraid."

"You're right. I know a story which Jesus told to people who didn't want to hear him: There was once a man who was very rich. He dressed in the richest clothes and ate only the very best food. Every day was a feast in his house and he just lived to eat, drink, and have a good time. He couldn't think of anything else; his eyes were blind to whatever happened around him. He just loved himself. . . ."

"Didn't he even love his wife?"

"The story doesn't say whether he had a wife or not, but if he was so selfish he would not have loved his wife either. Perhaps she was a poor lonely woman because he just thought about feasting and rich meals."

"Did he eat all alone?"

"No, there were always many people around making noise, laughing, and eating with him. Otherwise, he would have been bored and he would have been afraid. They came just to eat like gluttons. They didn't come out of friendship. This man, this glutton, didn't see that a beggar who was so poor, so sick, and so weak that the dogs licked his wounds with their tongue was lying at the gate of his house."

"Did the dogs have pity on him?"

"Yes, sometimes dogs can sense it when a person is helpless.

Maybe the beggar had patted them on the head. But when they licked him he couldn't hold them back."

"They wanted to help. But was it good for his wounds?"

"The beggar's name was Lazarus and he had just one wish. He wanted to eat what fell from the table of the glutton so that he could satisfy his hunger."

"You read about what fell from the table."

"What did fall, Mommy?"

"I believe whatever was left on the dishes. When the glutton didn't want any more he pushed his plate away even if there was something still on it and this is what Lazarus hoped to get. Now it happened that the beggar died and he was carried by angels to the bosom of Abraham. . . ."

"Why didn't he go to heaven?"

"Just think back. What was the state of heaven after Adam and Eve were sent out of paradise?"

"Closed, completely closed."

"Yes, just as it is in the song, 'For the gate was closed until the Saviour stepped forth!' "

"But Jesus was there!"

"Yes, Jesus was there. But only his death could save the people. Jesus died and he took all the sins and hateful things of people on himself. But at the time of the rich glutton Jesus had not come."

"Did Jesus say that everything bad was his fault?"

"No," but he said, 'I am dying for the people,' just as if all these sins were his own. 'God the Father will forgive me for all the people and that will open up heaven again. When the people die they won't have to wait as Abraham did. They will go directly to heaven if they believe in me.' "

73

"Where was Abraham waiting?"

"The Israelites believed that Abraham and the just were waiting in some place other than hell. This place was peaceful and joyful just between heaven and hell. That is why Lazarus went to Abraham and Abraham received him and pressed him close to his heart as if he were a sick child."

"And where were the bad people?"

"They went to another place. That was hell and they were also waiting there, not in joyful rest but in unrest and pain, plagued by their unhappy conscience."

Manuel said suddenly, "I know! These two places were very near each other but they were separated by a deep pit, like a crevice in a glacier!"

"But much deeper and more terrible so that one simply couldn't cross over. Later the rich glutton also died and he went to this place of pain where he had to suffer terribly. Among other things he had a thirst which was more terrible than hunger."

"It was like when I have a fever, wasn't it?"

"Yes, but much worse. The glutton looked up and suddenly he saw Lazarus on the bosom of Abraham. He called out, 'O father, Abraham, send Lazarus to me that he may cool my tongue with water from the tip of his finger. . . .'"

"Was his tongue hot?"

"Yes, he was suffering from a thirst which he could not bear, and one tiny drop of water would have been wonderful. . . ."

"How did he know it was Lazarus when he hadn't paid attention to any of the people who had been around him?"

"Oh, he saw them all right. He just didn't want to take notice of them. They bothered him. They made him uncomfortable, irritable. Certainly, he knew about them. It is that much worse if he drove them out of his heart and thoughts."

"Sometimes when I am playing and you call me to come in to wash my hands I say, 'She's not calling, no, she's not calling. I don't hear a thing. I want to keep playing.'"

"Yes, exactly! One can also say, 'I don't see the misfortune near me because if I do I shall be obliged to do something about it. I shall have to help. But that will disturb me, I think.'"

"Full of pain the rich glutton called to Abraham who answered, 'Think, my son. In life you had joy and Lazarus knew only misery. Now he has comfort and you have pain. Besides, between us and you there is an impassable gulf. Even if one wanted to, he could not come over to you, and you could never come over to us.'"

"Lazarus couldn't go into hell to help?"

"No, he couldn't. He couldn't go to the rich glutton and the glutton couldn't come to him."

"And supposing God wanted it?"

"Then, yes, but this remains God's secret about which we know nothing or very little. We can only believe that God knows all things, that he can do and actually does all things which are necessary. Listen to the glutton as he called, 'I beseech you, O father Abraham, send Lazarus to the house of my parents. I have five brothers. Let him warn them so that they will not come to this place of suffering.'

Lazarus was supposed to go to his brothers to warn them and to tell them that as a dead man he had seen the glutton, their brother, languishing in hell. They would believe him and change their way of life. Abraham answers, 'They have Moses and the prophets. Let them heed them. They will hardly believe one coming from the kingdom of the dead.' "

"Mommy, do you mean the Moses who came to the Red Sea and then led the Jews out of Egypt?"

"Exactly. This is just what Abraham meant. How often had Moses shown the people the right path. Remember when he came from the mount of Sinai and broke the tables of the commandments?"

"Yes, I know."

"Tell me one of the commandments."

"Do not kill."

"How strange that this particular commandment came to your mind first. The same thing happened to your brothers. Do you know any other?"

" 'I am the Lord your God.' Or, 'Do not lie!' "

"Now you understand what Abraham meant."

"Yes, people are supposed to love God, the one God, and they shouldn't tell a lie or kill or . . . steal, or be jealous or curse."

"And what did the prophets have to say?"

"What is a prophet?" asks David.

"Someone who knows what is going to happen," answers Isabel.

"Right. The prophets foretold the coming of the Saviour long, long before he came. They told the people to stop doing evil, to have a good heart, and to wait for the Messiah with joy. But woe to those who would not believe in the Messiah.

"Woe to those who preferred an evil heart to a good one."

"Woe to those who turned their back on God and forgot him."

"They would be punished just like the glutton, Mommy?"

"Just like the glutton."

"Mommy, why wouldn't the rich man's brothers believe Lazarus even if he had returned from the dead? Why didn't God try to make them good again?"

"But, my darling, he did try, but not with the beggar Lazarus. I believe that Abraham was right. The people would not have believed. They had seen miracles but were not affected by them."

"When did God try to make them good, Mommy?"

"What did we read yesterday?"

"I know, Mommy, when the son of the widow died."

"Yes, the young man in the village of Nain. Think of the poor woman. She had lost her husband and had an only son whom she loved above all else. Now this son died. Jesus met the sad funeral procession. The young man was lying on a stretcher and covered with a cloth. . . ."

"Didn't they want a coffin?"

"No, they didn't have one. People were buried very quickly after they died on account of the decomposition which set in due to the heat. Most of the time they were buried in a cave."

"What is decomposition, Mommy?"

"When the body no longer has a soul and the heart doesn't beat any more and the blood doesn't flow through the veins, the body decays. . . ."

"Decay is bad, very bad. I don't want to see it!"

"Why? First of all, a body doesn't decay immediately, and if I thought you were to die I would hold your little dead body in my arms with just as much love as I do now. Do you think I would be disgusted?"

"No, because it's still me!"

77

"And if I were to die, I would still be your mother, and after a few days you would bury me without any feeling of revulsion. . . ."

"Melanie's baby looked like blue soap."

"But how pretty he looked among all the flowers."

"But he wasn't alive."

"No, how could the child be alive? But he is now living with God. He is living and so happy. He was dead but still he was the same child which had come from Melanie's body only five months before. We mustn't be afraid of death, darling."

"No, I'm not afraid, but dead people seem to be so far away. They are so serious. Death is so strong and stern, Mommy."

"But Jesus was stronger than death. When he saw the poor mother in Nain, he pitied her because she cried and walked so heartbrokenly behind the stretcher. 'Don't cry,' Jesus said to the woman. He wanted to console her. She was a mother like his own mother. The woman raised her head and stood still. Jesus went to the stretcher. The stretcher-bearers stopped, too, as did the many people accompanying the sad procession. No one spoke a word. They sensed that something incomprehensible was taking place before their very eyes. 'Young man, I say to you, arise.' Before anyone could get excited, the young man sat up, looked around him, and the winding cloth dropped down. His mother hurried up to him and they put their arms around each other so lovingly. They were together again and so happy! But the mother looked immediately at Jesus. She thought, just as did the people around, that a great prophet was among them. They all started giving praise to God. But, you know, they thought that Elijah the prophet was back. Elijah had lived in the neighborhood of Nain and he had also brought the young son of a widow back to life from the dead. He had said, 'O Lord, God of Sabaoth, help me to restore life to this boy. Give me the power to bring him back to life.' Jesus simply said, 'Young man, *I* say to you, arise.' Because he was the Son of God he could do this by himself. That's the difference. . . ."

"And what did the people say?"

"They went around telling the story everywhere. Many wanted to see Jesus and to listen to him, but they couldn't believe that he was the Messiah for whom they had been waiting. No, they just couldn't."

"And what about the little girl who was sleeping?"

"Which little girl do you mean, the little daughter of Jairus?"

"Yes."

"The child was so sick that she was going to die, when her despairing father hurried to Jesus. She was not yet dead. Jesus followed the father, but he was delayed while he was on his way to the little girl, and the father whose name was Jairus stood there wringing his hands anxiously and even impatiently."

"Just as you did when Andrew had a pain in his stomach and the doctor didn't come right away!"

"I'll tell you afterwards why Jesus was delayed. When Jesus and Jairus came to the house where the daughter lay, a servant came and called to them, 'Sir, your daughter is already dead. The Master Jesus does not have to come.' See how kindly Jesus looked at the poor father. He said to him, 'Don't be afraid, Jairus. Just believe. Believe that I can help your daughter to be well again.' He took Jairus and his wife, as well as his apostles Peter, James, and John, with him into the house to the child. He sent the others away. 'The child is not dead,' he said. 'She is just sleeping.'"

"Why did Jesus always say someone was sleeping if that person was really dead?"

"Because Jesus is the conqueror of death. He is stronger than death and he knew it. He also knew that he would one day rise from his own death. So he could say, 'She is sleeping.' He knew about life after death, but the people could only see that the girl was dead.

"They heard the mourners and the flute players who came only because someone was dead. They were paid for that. Each new person who arrived to visit was greeted by new wailing and music. . . ."

"Mommy, perhaps Jesus didn't want the people to notice it."

"What shouldn't they notice?"

"That he brought the girl back from the dead. That is why he says to them that she was sleeping. They would go away much faster and leave Jesus in peace."

"I think so, too. There were many people there because Jairus was rich and well off. He was a leader in the synagogue and temple. He was one of the Jews who helped to conduct divine service in the synagogue."

"Was he a sacristan?"

"No, he was more than a sacristan. He was also a teacher and he taught the children to read the scriptures."

"And because he was so rich, did so many mourners and flute players come just to earn some money?"

"Many also came because they found it interesting. There are always people like that. Jesus sent these people away! 'She is only sleeping,' he said. The crowd grumbled and insulted him. 'Sleeping, is she! She is as dead as a doornail. Can you beat that!'"

"Do you think the father of the girl knew that Jesus had brought the widow's son back to life?"

"No, I don't think so. I think that he was simply beside himself because his only daughter had died and he wanted to try this 'Master' about whom so much was said. I think he would have been ashamed to go to Jesus, too, if he had not been so upset. He wanted to try everything.

"The child was lying in bed. The door was closed. The weeping parents, the three apostles and Jesus stood around the bed. It was very still as Jesus took the child by the hand. . . ."

"Like the young man. . . ."

"And he said, 'Little girl, I say to you, arise!' —And the little girl stood up. The parents took her into their arms, crying for joy and trembling with excitement. In a short time she had been taken from them and then given back. 'Give her something to eat,' Jesus commanded. . . ."

"You're happy too because I can eat again after I was sick!"

"How prudent Jesus was to say simply to the parents, 'Give her something to eat.' How quickly the mother went about getting something for her and how happy her father looked as his little girl put bread into her mouth and drank from her cup the way she did before she was sick. But Jesus forbade them to tell what happened."

"What did the apostles say?"

"The Bible doesn't say. But they must have loved and admired Jesus very much. How very much they believed in him and how gladly they would lay down their lives for him who could do such things and who let them be around when he was doing them!"

81

"If a person believes as hard as he can, Mommy, does he always get his wish?"

"No, only when God thinks best. But sometimes God asks for a very strong faith, and even when there seems to be no hope, we must believe. Then miracles will happen. Do you know why Jesus was delayed as he was on his way to Jairus's house?"

"No."

"Do you remember the woman who was so sick for twelve long years?"

"Oh, yes, what did she have?"

"You know where children grow in the mother. The woman had a pain in this little hollow and she was suffering very much."

"Did she have any children?"

"She couldn't have any little boys and girls. She had a wound in that little hollow and it bled all the time and it wouldn't heal over. She became very weak. She had already gone to many doctors but it hadn't helped a bit. She had spent most of her money and still she didn't get better. Twelve years is a long time."

"As old as Manuel?"

"Yes, as long as Manuel has been in the world, just so long did the poor woman suffer. She had heard about the Master. She had heard that he could cure anything, that he knew everything. But she was afraid to come too near him. She was ashamed to tell what she had. . . ."

"I never tell the teacher when I have to go!"—

"But it would be all right to tell her. . . ."

"I don't like to. I would rather wait. I don't mind letting you, but the woman is like me because she doesn't want to say either!"

"She thought, —If I could only touch the hem of his gown I would be cured. That's why she always went with the people who followed Jesus. They pushed and shoved from front and back. Everyone wanted to see the master as closely as possible. Thanks be to God, now she was up front near Jesus and she succeeded in touching his gown believing firmly in her heart that she would be cured. She was cured immediately. She felt like a new person. But Jesus asked, 'Who touched me?' The people had been pushing so that Peter answered, 'They're crowding from all sides. How could one ever find the one who touched you. It wasn't us!' But Jesus wasn't referring to the pushing. He merely said, 'Someone has touched me and power has gone out from me.' "

"Like magic, Mommy!"

"No, a power which went out to the woman. The faith of the woman had relied on the power of Jesus. He felt it and wanted to know who touched him. 'I,' said the woman trembling. 'Forgive me, Master. It was I. Forgive my daring, but I believed that only you could heal me. I have been suffering for twelve years. Only you, Master,'—and she threw herself at his feet. And in spite of her tears, she smiled happily and gratefully. 'Thank you, Master, and have pity on me.' "

"The apostles were quite puzzled and the crowd was silent. But Jesus only looked at her and said, 'Take comfort, my daughter. Your faith has helped you. Go in peace.' He consoled her. He strengthened her faith for the rest of her life. He calmed her. Perhaps he would have said still more if the servant of

Jairus had not come. That's the way it was. Then they hurried to the dead child, who was sleeping."

"Gee! Mommy, but the woman was brave to tell Jesus it was she. And in front of everybody!"

"Think about this the next time I ask you, 'David, did you do that?' Think about the woman and her courage and say, 'Yes, I did,' and then explain immediately just how it happened. This is the way you'll have to do later when you go to confession. It's quite simple. Jesus will ask you, 'How did it happen, David?' "

"But he already knows!"

"Yes, he does, but he just wants you to know so that you can tell him about it. . . ."

"Because I'll have a lump otherwise. . . ."

"Where will you have a lump?"

"In my throat. When I lie I always have a lump in my throat and it beats like crazy. . . ."

"That's your heart. But when you tell the truth your heart beats, too. . . ."

"But without a lump."

"That's your conscience as well."

"The voice inside? That's your voice, Mommy!"

"And the fear?"

"I'm afraid of God. When I'm afraid, it's always God."

"And Jesus?"

"I'm not afraid of Jesus. I say, 'Forgive me,' or, 'Please,' or, 'Thank you.' . . ."

"But we do the same to God!"

"God is like Papa and Jesus is like you!"

"And the Holy Spirit?"

"You two together...."

"But you know you must love God above all things...."

"I do."

"And God is God the Father, God the Son, and God the Holy Spirit."

"That is what I meant, Mommy, really it is."

Is God always good?

Cain and Abel. A good disposition, a bad disposition. Envy. Is God unfair? Sin lurks just in front of the door. Fratricide. All evil can lead to death. Evil as a consequence of original sin. A mother loves her children even when they do naughty things. The mother of God loves us. God is unfathomable. God curses Cain. He knows all things. He is good. The salvation of mankind in God's plan. Is God never evil when he allows evil to happen? Earthquake in Africa. Slaughter of innocent people. We should not tempt God. Belief in God and eternal life. A struggle of faith. The obedience of Abraham. Abraham's hospitality. The three men and Abraham. Issac's birth is prophesied. Abraham is asked by God to sacrifice Isaac. Abraham's tremendous obedience. God does not accept the sacrifice. Job. God gives Job into the hands of the devil. Job's terrible trials. Job's faith. Job's reward. God takes and God gives.

AFTER we had read the story of the first fratricide, Isabel said, "Why didn't God like Cain's sacrifice the way he liked Abel's? Cain brought his offering, too."

"I think Cain offered his sacrifice with an indifferent disposition."

"But that isn't in the Bible."

86

"Yes, it is. Cain took what was next best for the sacrifice and Abel took the very best for God."

"How did they know that God was pleased with one but not with the other?"

"We don't know. Abel was always gay. His sheep were always splendid. He was happy, polite, glad to help. Cain was morose and he had a poor disposition. He didn't do much to improve himself. Instead, he grumbled inside and envied Abel. He was unhappy and most likely lonely. Perhaps he hadn't done his work well and a poor harvest depressed him. He fed his heart on these misfortunes and said to himself, 'There it is. Abel stands in God's favor and I don't!' But God wants to help him. 'Why are you so angry, Cain? Why do you scowl so at the earth? When you do good you will find favor, but if you think only about evil, sin lurks just before the door. You should be master of yourself.' But Cain didn't want to be master of himself. His envy and anger, dark brothers of hate, misled him and he murdered Abel. Every evil thought, every envious thought, is a step in the direction of evil."

"But we don't kill, we just quarrel."

"But you said once in a rage, 'Peter ought to be killed.' "

"Because he made me so furious and I wasn't to blame!"

"Not completely. Because Adam and Eve disobeyed God, your anger, your uncontrolled temper, are results of this first sin."

"How terrible! Eve had a murderer for a son. He killed her other son. Did she love Cain any more?"

"What do you think?"

"I think she always loved him but that she was terribly sad."

"Parents love their children forever . . . come what may. I would like to say something else to you. There are some things

87

in life and even in the Bible which seem unfair but we don't know God's reason. We don't know what is in his mind. Why must a child suddenly be run over? Why was Cain not pleasing to God? Why did Job have to put up with so much? All that we know is: God knows better."

"You don't always cut the cake evenly either."

"What do you mean?"

"You just cut pieces as they come!"

"Don't you think that's all right?"

"I used to think it was funny. Now I think it's all right that the pieces are cut just as they come!"

"I mean that people shouldn't let themselves be tempted into saying to God, 'It isn't fair. God is unfathomable.' We know only a few things and then not too much about them. Every day we should pray for faith and trust."

"Did Eve cry, Mommy, when Abel died?"

"Yes, she did. Perhaps she even said to Adam, 'It's our fault. We're the ones who were disobedient.'"

"What did Cain do then?"

"He was cursed by God."

"Did he go back home?"

"No, he ran away. When I was small my mother told me a story which made a great impression on me. After Cain had killed his brother he hid himself. He didn't want to hear God's voice any more. He wanted to get out of God's sight."

"Out of God's sight?"

"Yes, he hid in the deepest cave he could find and still he could see in the dark God's eyes, reminding him of the terrible thing he had done. He tried to flee from those eyes but when he thought God couldn't see him any more, God's eyes still stared at him. Cain screamed, hid, and buried himself in holes in the ground, but when he opened his eyes he knew God was still watching him."

"That's because God knows everything, everything people do. He knows when I hit Peter and even when I think that I would like to hit him."

"Try not to kill, Peter, even with angry thoughts. They are as bad as evil words and deeds. Try, David."

"Mommy, is God always good?"

"Yes, always!"

"Is he never bad? He is the one who invented evil."

"I said that God knows everything, the good and the bad. But he doesn't wish evil for people and nature."

"But you said he knew that people wouldn't obey."

"Yes, and that's why he planned the salvation of mankind. When I, for example, don't allow you to go near fire, I'm wondering sometimes what I would do if you didn't obey, or how I could make you see the danger. Perhaps I let you get a tiny burn. That hurts me as much as it hurts you, but you must learn to keep away from fire."

"Then sometimes you're bad to me just like God is to people."

"Do you really think I'm bad?"

"Yes, you're bad, too!"

"Supposing you fell into fire and burned yourself terribly because I hadn't warned you enough or because I hadn't told you what fire can do, would that be better? Do you like to be in a hospital? Do you remember the time you fell off the wall? I had forbidden you to climb up on it. But you did it just the same. You fell and had to have surgery."

Manuel is silent. "But does God," he continued stubbornly, "punish even babies who are in the crib?"

I am at a loss for words. "What do you mean? Explain yourself."

"Yes, in the earthquake in Africa. Did only disobedient people die?"

"No, certainly not, darling Manuel. What happened there was terrible. But we may not question God the way you're doing. You can't tempt God, it says in the Bible. We don't know why God allows such things to happen. We don't know what is in God's mind."

"What about the babies who died in Agadir? Are they with God now?"

"Yes."

"Why?"

"Because they had finished their life on this earth."

"But is their mother dead?"

"Perhaps not."

"Is she crying?"

"Terribly."

"Would you cry if we died?"

"Of course, very much."

"Would we be with God, too?"

"Yes."

"Right away or only after a while?"

"Perhaps right away, perhaps after a while. . . ."

"Would you be happy?"

"I would have to keep telling myself how well off you are with God although I would feel so alone. I would be a poor inconsolable mother."

"Would you love God just the same?"

"Yes, I would in spite of it all because I believe that he knows best and that I must obey him. Think about Abraham and his little son Isaac. Do you think this old father didn't love his child?"

"Why do you say 'old'?"

"Sarah, Abraham's wife, had no little boy for a long time. When they were old, like real old grandparents, three men came to see them one evening. Abraham had never seen them before. He was sitting in front of his tent but he stood up immediately and extended them the hospitality for which they asked. Do you know what that hospitality meant? It meant inviting the people into the tent, giving up their beds, letting them sit by the fire during the night, giving them food, —roasted calf or cake, cheese, honey, their precious water for drinking, for washing...."

"Why was water so precious?"

"Because they had to haul it up out of a deep well and water was scarce. That was hospitality. The aging Sarah had to do a great deal of coming and going for all her ninety years. The strangers were angels but Abraham didn't know it. When they left the next day they thanked him very much and then they told Abraham a secret...."

"What kind of a secret?"

"That his wife would have a little son very soon. But when

91

Abraham told Sarah she burst out laughing and said, 'I'm already old, much too old, and so are you.' But nine months later she bore a son, Isaac. That is a lovely Hebrew name and means *to laugh out of joy*. You know how grandparents love and spoil their grandchildren, don't you? And you can imagine the joy of these old parents when they looked at the beautiful little curly-headed Isaac who grew from day to day and helped them so much. There was always someone there, and Abraham could think proudly and happily that one day Isaac would marry and then he would be surrounded with grandchildren. But now the terrible part comes. 'Abraham,' called God. 'Here I am,' he answered. 'Take this beloved son of yours, Isaac,' God said to him. 'Go to the high mountain Moriah and there sacrifice him to me.' What do you suppose Abraham felt as his heart cried out, 'No, Lord, not my child, my beloved child!' But he went to the mountain. He took some wood with him. He did want to obey God. The child jumped here and there and was delighted to be taking a walk. Once in a while he asked, 'Where is the victim for the sacrifice, father? What are you going to offer, father?' Abraham didn't answer. He went on farther but it was night in his heart. Abraham stacked the wood which he had brought and then he tied his son's hands behind his back. Isaac resisted, cried out, begged and pleaded with his father. He just couldn't understand what his father was going to do. But Abraham raised his knife, ready to do the most terrible thing, ready to offer to God what he loved most, his cherished son. But the arm holding the knife remained raised, held firmly by an angel. 'No, Abraham, stop. Take this ram and offer it to me instead,' God said. 'I wanted to test you to see how much you loved me. But you did not hesitate. You were ready to offer Isaac and that is enough. I want you to know one thing—your descendants, that is, your children's children, will be as numerous as the sands of the sea.' "

"Abraham believed the word of God unconditionally. Do you understand that? I must tell you one more story, the story of Job. Let's look at the picture Bible."

"Is he sick?" asks Peter.

"He is sick. He has leprosy, the most terrible disease of the time because it was incurable and very contagious. Now lepers can be cured sometimes, but leprosy decays the body. It disfigures limbs and faces. Everyone was afraid of the people who had it. Lepers used to carry a clapper which they had to use when people came near them. Everyone fled as they approached."

"Are there still lepers?"

"Yes, but I shall tell you about them tomorrow."

"But let's hear about Job. One day the angels of God gathered before the heavenly Father, and Satan, the fallen angel, was also present. 'Where do you come from?' God asked. The devil answered, 'I have been roaming over the earth.' 'Have you seen my servant Job?' asked God. 'There is no one like him in the whole world. No one is as honest as he is or as Godfearing. No one avoids evil as he does.' 'That is no great thing,' the devil answered. 'Haven't you given him everything,—a house, children, herds, and good things of all kinds? Why shouldn't he honor you? But try him. Take away all that he has and then see what he does. . . .' God said to Satan, 'All that he has is in your hands. Take all that he owns, but you may make no attempt on his life.'

"The unhappy Job now underwent many terrible experiences. He was robbed of his very large herds. You know, he had about four thousand sheep. His ten children were buried under the ruins of his house which collapsed while a feast was going on during a dust storm. Job grieved and tore his clothes, but he retained his confidence in God. 'The Lord has given. The Lord has taken. Blessed be the name of the Lord,' Job said.

"Satan didn't want to admit defeat. After all this Job became leprous, and since he had no house he had to sit on a dung heap probably because it was so cold at night. 'You must have committed some terrible sins if God punishes you like this,' said his angry wife, and so did his friends. 'Turn to God and die.' But Job answered, 'Haven't we received all the good things we have from God? Shouldn't we also accept the evil? I'm doing penance for many mistakes, but God will forgive me because I am suffering. I believe in God and I trust him. I will never curse his name.'

"Satan had to withdraw. He was beside himself because Job remained true to God and he expected no reward. And yet God did reward him before long. He gave Job back double his former riches and ten children again among whom were three lovely daughters. He lived to be one hundred and forty years old and lived with his children, his grandchildren, and his great grandchildren.

"We don't know what God had in mind for Agadir. Why was this town blotted out? Why did ten thousand people have to die? Why did so many of those left have to grieve? We can only believe that God knows what he is doing and why he is doing what he does. We can only believe that he is the father of us all and though he allowed these people to die so terribly, yet he took them to himself. We must, after the example of Abraham and Job, be obedient and trust even when it is most difficult."

Mrs. S. always holds her
collection money up high!

Shrove Tuesday at home. Ash Wednesday. Resolution. Lenten sacrifices. Children and eating in Lent. The real sacrifice in daily life. Prayer. Our own imperfection. You're always patient, Mommy. Fasting which goes unnoticed. A story about St. Francis and Lent.

YESTERDAY we had a wonderful feast. Peter decorated the children's room with paper streamers, Chinese lanterns, and painted wrapping paper on the walls. He put a table for pastry in the corner of the room. All the children were masked as were their father and I! We laughed a great deal, ate doughnuts, played endless rounds of 'going to Jerusalem,' and concluded with a raffling game. The children were hilarious with extraordinary ideas. The whole thing was very successful!

On Ash Wednesday the children went quietly and recollectedly to Mass.

"Ashes on the head is something good," Manuel said. "I got a lot."

"Me, too," said Isabel. "Look!"

David adds, "I've torn off two buttons as a sign that I'm sad because I'm made of dust!"

"Stop fooling," frowned Andrew. "You'll be dust soon enough!"

96

"In a coffin?" asked David innocently. "So many coffins in the cemetery and all full of dust? Do the people forget it so soon that our pastor has to remind us?"

Manuel oozes virtue! "On Good Friday no one is allowed to eat any fat, meat, or anything else."

"Oh, you martyr! And you won't even eat spinach which you just don't like!"

"Monica hoards chocolates in a box!"

"Yes, and then she gobbles them down by herself," Peter broke in.

"That's no sacrifice, especially not for you, my dear Peter. You don't like chocolates."

"Don't you want to let Manuel borrow your bike this afternoon?"

Peter blushed, swallowed, and said a little too cheerfully, "Sure, take it. You rat," he added hoarsely, "if anything happens to it, I'll punch you in the belly. Go ahead. Take it. It's at least a sacrifice. . . ."

I do not concur with those who stress giving up something at table. We eat so moderately that it seems senseless to talk any further about it. One would think we were in the Middle Ages and that we devoured a whole roasted ox at dinner. Other sacrifices which are more important retreat to the background. There are so many ways in which children can deny themselves. Isabel dreams of presents which have heroic size. "If a poor child should come some night, I'd give it my—oh, Mommy, what should I give? My coat? My coat goes to David. My apron? But you would scold. . . ."

"It is high time we say something about the real sacrifices of Lent. There is always something in daily living which one can give up, for instance quarreling, even if one is right. Empty the wastebasket without being told ten times to do so. Get up in the morning five minutes earlier and read something from the Gospel or the psalms. Isabel, spread Manuel's bed out when he goes to serve an early Mass and then don't tell me about it. Just do it! Manuel, let Ludwig serve more often on the right even if it's your turn, and don't make any fuss about it. Let Tony win once in a while when you're playing football, but don't let him know what you're doing. Think about his poor leg. Plan on some little thing which you can do during the whole Lenten season. And each evening before you go to bed you can kneel down alone in front of your bed and say a short prayer for the people in Asia. Do what you do without letting others know you are doing it. Keep your head high. Be happy. Don't let your behavior give evidence of sacrifice."

"But Mrs. S. always holds her money for the collection basket very high between her two fingers so that everyone can see!"

Oh, he is so right. I see it, too. But how can I set the little Pharisee right, especially when he is watching me so closely and I want so much to break out into a laugh?

"Oh, we mustn't bother about that. We have enough with our own imperfections,—my impatience, for example. . . ."

All five looked at me horrified. "But you're very patient."

"No," I reply, "I'm human like you and I make mistakes."

"You don't make mistakes. You're wonderful."

"I'm your mother and that is wonderful, not I."

But they didn't want to believe under any circumstance that I was anything but a model of perfection. I tried to make them understand about my daily struggle, at the same time not surrendering an inch of my authority.

The Lenten season is a time for moderation, for self-control.

"You can think better if you don't eat too much," says Isabel.

"That time I was sick and couldn't eat I thought up all kinds of stories."

"The prophets fasted. . . ."

"So that they could have ideas. . . ."

"I didn't mean that. I meant that they did this out of discipline, out of self-denial. But the prophets also knew from experience that they could talk better with God, that they hear God better, that they sometimes came nearer to God when they fasted."

"But that can also weaken a person," Peter said soberly. "If someone is hungry, he gets cross!"

"But if a person holds out, it doesn't seem so hard, and then God often gives a person a lot of grace, Peter."

"We don't want to be proud of what we do in Lent. . . ."

"I want to tell you another story. In the convent of St. Francis of Assisi there was a Brother who found the Lenten fast very hard, so hard that he could not stand it any longer. But as he didn't want to sin, by eating in secret, he went with his problem to St. Francis and confessed everything to him. St. Francis listened to the story, reassured the Brother, and ordered a table to be set with many good things. Then he invited the Brother to eat without any interference."

"How nice!" exclaimed Isabel.

"Yes, but wait and see what happens. Do you know what St.

Francis did? He sat down with the Brother and they ate together. Why do you suppose he did that?"

"Maybe he was hungry, too," said David.

"So that the Brother would not be eating alone, so that the Brother would not have to be ashamed," said Andrew.

"You've guessed it!"

I believe that in this case the real sacrifice for St. Francis was breaking his own fast. But he did it out of love for the unhappy and somewhat weak Brother.

"Keep your resolution this Lent modestly, without making any fuss about it remembering that Easter follows Lent. Joy follows sadness and darkness precedes the light. That is our hope."

Are there still people as poor as Lazarus?

The friends of Jesus. The Christians. We ought to love one another. The near missions. To obey and to love. Andrew and the little pusher. Guilt and atonement. Freedom. The reward in education. Hunger in the world. Why don't they have any-thing to eat? Our share of help for the underdeveloped countries. Go and teach all nations. The missions. The merciful Samaritan. What is a Levite? Was it a high priest? What is a Samaritan? Who is my neighbor? Love the Lord your God with your whole heart. Mommy, I don't love myself. Love of God. Love of neighbor. Should I forgive? Fit of rage. Forgiveness.

"You are the friends of Jesus. You are baptized. You are Christians. You bless yourselves with the sign of the cross. All Christians and baptized people in the whole world do this."

"Are there many Christians in the world, Mommy?"

"Yes, there are many, but everyone should come to know and learn to love Jesus. They can do this only if they see that the friends of Jesus are good to one another, that they love one another, that they help one another. Before Jesus died, he said to his friends, 'My little children, I'll still be with you a little while. I'm giving you a new commandment. Love one another as I have loved you. That is how everyone will know that you are my disciples, that you are my friends, if you love one another.'

101

Andrew, you have already been a disciple of Jesus for eight years. . . ."

"And me, Mommy?"

"Stop and think."

"Eight years, too!"

"No. How old are you? You are six!"

"Six years! I've been a disciple for as long as I've been alive, —six years!"

"No, you've been a disciple only for as long as you've been baptized."

"But only babies are baptized."

"No, even grown-ups are baptized. There are people who have never heard of Jesus. Then you come along and tell them about Jesus and you show them that you follow his commandments, that you try to be good. Then these people say, 'This boy Peter really serves the true God. We want to obey and serve Jesus too.'"

"And love him, too."

"That's right. We are very happy to serve and to obey someone we love."

"Not always. I love you, Mommy," said Andrew, "but I don't always think it's nice when you say 'Come in now. Pick up your things,' and just when I'm in the middle of the nicest fun!"

"But I call you to come in only in the evening when it gets cool and you could get sick. I call you in because you need sleep. You would get sick if you didn't have enough sleep. Naturally, it is unpleasant when you have to stop in the middle of something. But I always give you plenty of time. Don't you understand? What kind of a mother would I be if I didn't look

102

out for you, if I didn't care for each of you? You know and you believe that I want to protect you. Just so must we believe God and trust him. When he calls us, when he asks something, —something that we don't like in the least, we must obey."

"Lend Erwin my scooter?" Peter wanted to know. "But I don't think he's very nice at all. He's always copying!"

"Mommy, I want to whisper something to you. Peter, don't you listen! Mommy," —Andrew digs into his pocket, "I know where my little spoon is!"

"Where?"

"In my pocket. It went in here because it didn't want to eat for me anymore...."

"And now, Andrew?"

"Now it wants to eat again because I want it too!"

Andrew wanted to eat the way the grown-ups do and he didn't like the idea of a children's spoon. He just simply let it disappear. Now in his own way he tried to make the matter good.

"Now I don't have to seek any more, Andrew. I have looked just about everywhere for it!"

"I know, Mommy, I love you very much. And now my little spoon is here again!" Baffling logic! How much it must have cost him to make his own all that I had said about obeying and loving so that he could overcome his dislike for the spoon.

"Know what, Andrew? On Sunday you may eat with a regular spoon because you're a big boy. And then on weekdays you'll use it because it makes me happy...."

"And because he can eat better with it. Otherwise, he'll be using his fingers," put in Peter realistically.

"Mommy, I'd like to know something else," chimed in Andrew who wanted so much to talk about something else.

"Tell me, are there poor people today like Lazarus who sat at the gate of the rich glutton?"

"Of course there are. In India and in Africa you can meet such poor people on the street, dressed in rags and terribly thin. . . ."

"Are they hungry?"

"They're hungry and have been hungry for so long that when they get something to eat they become deathly sick. Look at this picture in the newspaper of the Congo. See the Negro boy who sits near his mother!"

"Why is his mother lying on the ground?"

"Because she can't walk any more. Her strength is all gone."

"And doesn't the boy cry?"

"The poor boy has already cried so much from fear and hunger that he can't cry any more. He just waits. Maybe he'll also lie down on the ground near his mother under the hot African sun and they will both die together."

"Isn't there anything anywhere to buy or anything to eat in the fields or on the trees?"

"If they want to buy something they need money. But they can get money only if they can work for it. They have to be given things first, —a plow and tools and machinery so that they can work. They must be helped. They must learn to read so that they can work the machines."

104

"Who is supposed to help?"

"We, all of us in the world, Germans, French, Russians, Americans, Swiss, Austrians, Poles. . . . If things are going well for us in our own country and out there in Africa poor starving boys are sitting near starving mothers, then we are like the rich glutton. We know that Lazarus is sitting at the gate waiting for what falls from the table, but we just simply forget this. Look, I have to take care of you, Papa and I, because God has given you to us and has said, 'I am giving you this child. Bring him up right. Teach him to love me. Teach him to work and to help others.' We have the responsibility. You know, we have the task of protecting you and caring for you. If we don't do that we are very guilty before God and you. But we belong to the world and we forget this all the time. We belong to the peoples of the earth. Shortly before Jesus ascended into heaven he said to his disciples, 'There will come a time when I shall be with you no longer. You know the good news. You know that I am your Saviour, your Messiah, who opened heaven for you and forgives you your sins. You know that and you believe in me. You know what mercy, goodness, and readiness to help other people means.

" 'But through you the other people in the world must come to know God and his Son and the new commandment of Jesus, his new commandment of love. Therefore go into the whole world and announce my good news to all peoples. Whoever believes and is baptized will be saved. Whoever does not believe will be damned.' We believe Jesus. Shouldn't we then not also go to all people to help them?"

"But that's what John [a friend of ours who is a priest in Africa] does."

"Yes, that's what John is doing, but one is not enough for so much work. We all must help not only the missionaries of the world but also all who are not priests. . . ."

"Once upon a time there was a man who went from Jerusalem to Jericho. This was a very unpleasant road, about twenty-five miles long, something like the distance from Lindau to Meersburg. . . ."

"That's a long way!"

"Yes, but the way to Meersburg leads through a road which is like a garden where you can meet people. This way from Jerusalem to Jericho led through a mountainous, very lonely stretch of land which was like a desert. There were only rocks, sand, and in between a narrow winding path. . . ."

"Like the Alps?"

"No, it was narrower, barer, and more sinister. There were many robbers hiding in the rocks and they used to fall on wanderers robbing them of everything they had. This man was travelling the dangerous road and he actually did fall into robbers' hands. They seized him and took all he had. They didn't even leave him his own clothes. They beat him and then ran away. . . ."

"Because they were afraid they might be caught. They had a bad conscience."

"And then they left the man lying there half dead."

"A real true robber story, Mommy!" David was blissfully happy and the cruelty of the situation did not touch him. Many children are like that and one should not be shocked by it.

"Maybe his wife and children were waiting for him to come home. Perhaps they were worried and crying while he lay on the ground bleeding and stripped of his clothes. Maybe he fainted, his head humming and aching. Maybe he was unable to move. He must have thought with panic about the coming ice-cold of the night. For the nights were as cold as the days were hot. Hence the people always went dressed in a light wool."

"Poor man," said David. "The robbers might have robbed him, but they didn't have to beat him."

"But robbing was against the law of Moses, the law of God."

"Yes, but robbers rob and that is their occupation."

"And supposing they were sorry?"

"Then they would have to bring everything back and stop being robbers."

"Just listen to what happened next. A priest came along this lonely path. He saw the poor man, looked, and kept going."

"Cheap!"

"I think the priest was afraid that the same thing would happen to him and so he hurried along faster."

"But he was a priest!"

"You're right, but a priest is human, too, and he has fear and needs."

"But that's like a coward."

"Yes, it was cowardly, but often we're cowards too."

"Now," said David, "what was he doing on the road? Shouldn't he have been in the temple?"

"But the priest couldn't stay in the temple all day long for services. He had other things to attend to. He had to visit his people, anoint the sick, bury the dead, take care of his family. . . ."

"And what about this priest?"

"He might have been going from Jerusalem to Jericho in order to perform a service in the temple. Priests had to do this twice a year because Jericho was a priestly city. After him came a Levite. Levites were assistants to the priest as well as keepers of the holy tabernacle, you know. Their duty was to tend this most sacred thing of the Jews which preserved the tablets of the Law and the manna. No one dared go inside. There was a curtain in the tabernacle and behind this curtain was the Ark of the Covenant in which these precious things were stored. The high priest was allowed to part the curtain once a year and to come very close to the Ark of the Covenant, and that means, very close to God. God spoke to the people in this room and he told them through the high priest what they should do."

"That was very nice, then. They knew everything!"

"Don't you always know what you should do?"

"Yes, I do, but to hear what God says is something different. I don't do that. But what is the Levite doing?"

"Oh, he did just what the priest did."

"Glutton, just like the glutton, Mommy! Why didn't they want to see?"

"Listen. A Samaritan who was riding along the road. . . ."

"What's a Samaritan?"

"A Samaritan is a person who belonged to the family of the Jews, too, but the Jews despised the Samaritans because they had separated themselves from the Jews. They celebrated their own religious services instead of going to Jerusalem to do this. They had also intermarried with the pagans and this horrified the Jews. The Samaritans were a sort of half Jew. They also looked for the Messiah and they believed in one God. The Jews called them the unclean. And just such a person came riding along the road towards Jericho. He saw the poor man and his heart filled with pity for him. . . ."

"The same way I feel sorry for the poor Negro lady...."

"The Samaritan climbed down off his beast, went over to the man who was lying on the ground, and he took oil and wine from his riding bag...."

"What did he do that for?"

"People always carried oil and wine because these things could be used for food as well as medicine. Wounds could be washed out with wine and the oil was used for ointment. The Samaritan took the bleeding man in his arms, lifted him up, and put him on his beast. Then they continued on to the nearest inn. He brought the poor man in, laid him on a bed, washed him, gave him food and drink, made him comfortable, bandaged his wounds and took care of him all night long."

"Just like you do when I'm sick."

"Yes, but I'm your mother and I've known you since you were born. The Samaritan took care of a stranger as if he were his neighbor or friend. As he was leaving to go about his own business the next day, the Samaritan said to the innkeeper, 'Take care of him and here is your money, two *denarii*.'"

"What are denarii?"

"Coins worth about forty cents."

"Is that a lot?"

"At that time it was. It was the pay a man received for working two days."

"Then the Samaritan told the innkeeper that if the money was not enough, he would pay more when he came back that way again. Which of the three showed that he was the poor man's neighbor? Who helped? Who listened to what his heart told him?"

"The last one, Mommy, the Samaritan...."

"Yes, the Samaritan, the man who was unclean, the man who didn't belong to the Jews, was the one who loved his neighbor the way Jesus wants you to."

"Who is my neighbor, Mommy?"

"A teacher of the Law asked Jesus the very same question and Jesus told him the story of the Samaritan."

"But his question was not an honest one. He just wanted to expose Jesus the way Peter does with his foolish questions!"

"Oh, I wouldn't judge him so quickly. The teacher had already asked Jesus, 'Master, what do I have to do to go to heaven?', and Jesus had answered, 'Tell me what the Law of Moses says.'"

"'You shall love the Lord your God with all your heart, with all your strength, and your neighbor as yourself.'"

"I just don't understand. How can a person love his neighbor?"

"Now listen well. You're supposed to love your neighbor the way you love yourself."

"But I don't love myself...."

"Really? Supposing we had only one sled for you and Daniel. Who would want it all the time?"

"I would. I'm bigger!"

"And who puts chocolate into his mouth so fast just so he won't have to share it?"

Silence.

"And who pushes others away from the stove because he wants to be warm?"

"Sometimes I do that..."

"And who pushes other children in the school out of the way when St. Nicholas has apples to give away? Who always wants to be first? No, not always you. All of us do things like that.

110

Who doesn't want to suffer when he's sick? Who whines immediately when he bumps into something?

"Who won't put up with thirst when he's taking a hike? Do you still think we don't love ourselves best? When there is a fire, people run away because they don't want to burn. Maybe we could think of others and help them. But, you know, in spite of this it is still right to look out for the body and to see to it that nothing happens because our body is a gift from God. Everything belongs to God. He wants us to take care of the body, but he doesn't want us to think only of our body. We mustn't serve the body as if everything rotated around it like . . ."

"Just like the Israelites danced around the golden calf which was wood inside."

"Exactly! Otherwise we would forget our neighbor whom we should love as we do ourselves. The Israelites thought that the most important thing was to love God and so they forgot their neighbor. But Jesus said to them, 'You can't love God if you don't love your neighbor.'"

"Does the Negro love me?"

"I think so, but that has nothing to do with it. If he's afraid and thinks you are bad, he might hurt you just to defend himself. But that still does not change matters. You are supposed to love the Negro, Peter, Rudy, and Jerry Moser."

"Him too? He's always hitting me!"

"Then get out of his way!"

"And if he looks me up?"

"Then be brave. And if he still hits you, try in the evening to forgive him. He is naughty—and poor. But if he fell off his bike and was lying there on the ground and you came along, would you leave him there because he is always pounding you?"

"No, I would help him, but I wouldn't be happy about it. He might even hit me again!"

"Yes, but Jesus would say to you, 'David, you have understood me. I'm in you and you're in me.'"

Manuel forgot himself today and went into a rage. I had thrown away a picture which he had painted. His grief was real and great, but his disappointment and anger over my thoughtlessness was even greater.

"But why did you throw it away?"

"Because it was all crumpled up on the floor."

"But it was for you," and he broke into a passionate flow of tears. "I don't want to talk to you for eight days. Yes, eight days long—long!"

I went out and closed the door. I was just as unhappy as he was, but I decided to wait until his rage subsided. Later he sat at table, without tears, obedient but silent.

"Won't you pray, please, Manuel."

"No, I don't want to pray," and then he pulled his napkin over his head. Peter smirked.

Father asked, "Manuel, what are you doing? We're waiting."

A tiny suppressed voice answered from under the white cloth, "I'm my own boss! I don't want to pray. . . ."

Muffled sobs could be detected in his voice. Peter prayed, Manuel just barely. His grieved look kept meeting mine and my heart was bleeding on account of his forlornness. I spoke quite naturally to him, undressed him, gave him his bath, dried him, combed his hair. But he continued silent and as one far away. At prayer time he knelt before me. His earnest little face did not look up at me as usual. "Forgive those who have done evil against you. Forgive them and be good to those who were not nice to you. Jesus says, 'Come to me all you who labor and are burdened and I will make you feel better. Come to me if you're sad and tired and I'll give you comfort. I am meek and humble of heart.'

"Let's be good to one another. I want to be good to you, Manuel, and you want to be good to me. Jesus was gentle. Let's be gentle with each other. 'Let the little ones come to me.' Go to Jesus and the hurt will go away from your heart. Jesus was very kind with little children. He will comfort you, too.

"Just say simply, 'Lord, I give you the crumpled drawing. Lord, I give you my sadness. Lord, comfort me.'"

Will God ask if I took the trouble?

A much loved person dies. Fear of death. A hard death. The mind of God. Alarming images of death. Eternal life. Thy kingdom come in the whole world. The task of a Christian. The good thief. We must always be ready. Pray for a good death.

A FRIEND lies before us in death. He was Andrew's confirmation godfather and has been like a close relative to the children. He was a dear upright man of seventy years. Although in many things he differed in point of view with our progressive eldest, for instance he thought all abstract art quite absurd, Andrew approached him full of respect. The children paid tribute to the fact that he was incapable of being bribed! They admired his integrity, his unqualified truthfulness, and even his simplicity.

I had told the children that Uncle Arnim was really very sick, that he was hovering between life and death, and that he would have to receive the last sacraments tonight.

The children were more subdued in their play—but only for a while. At prayer time David said dryly, "Perhaps he is already dead." Isabel shuddered perceptibly. Later I found her in bed, bathed in tears. "I keep seeing small lights and among them a very small one and death is standing near with a rake."

I carried her to my bed in order not to disturb the other children.

114

"I really don't think death is like that, Isabel. For reasons which we do not always know or understand God decides, 'I want this person to come to me. It is time for him.' And then he picks him like a flower."

"But why do some people die so hard, with so much pain and agony?"

"Perhaps it's the last test which God gives a person for his salvation. Perhaps the soul knows what is going on, but we can't know. Uncle Arnim will see God, but not the way he saw here on earth. God will talk with him. Yes, God will talk with him. When I was as small as you I couldn't picture to myself that God didn't have pity on people, that he didn't just simply love them. I couldn't imagine that he ever did anything wrong and this confidence has always remained with me."

"Mommy, I'm as afraid of death as if it were the devil!"

"No, darling, you're just picturing death the way you've seen it in the picture books,—a skeleton with a scythe, sinister and merciless. Death is also represented in another way in many fairy tales. It's something like a person who speaks and asks, or like one who comes, goes, and takes someone with him. Look, I've been afraid of death, too. I was afraid of it before the birth of a child, for instance. Confidence is the only thing which can help us. We should say to God, 'You are doing what is right. You are the Father. You are the Son. You are the Holy Spirit.' We must always keep this in mind. Only a person who does not know Christ is afraid of death. We go to God into eternal life if we obey him only by dying. Or we go into eternal perdition if we turned away from the will of God and deliberately sinned against his commands."

"But you told us yesterday at table that there are still some tribes of Africans who consider it a duty to kill their old father. Do they go immediately into hell?"

"No, I said it would be a sin if these people knew the commandments and then deliberately went against them. These Africans go according to the laws of their tribe.

"They don't know anything about Jesus. They follow their duty as sons. It is terrible and impossible for us, but for them it is right.

"But we must pray. 'Thy kingdom come.' That means that God should be the ruler of the whole world. 'Go and teach all nations. . . .' It means that God has sent his Son to us . . . that the Son of God redeemed us. We should pray that the priests, the Sisters, the Brothers, the teachers, the doctors, can help these Africans so that they too will be friends of Jesus. Maybe one day you'll take part in this missionary work. It's hard work because it's not sufficient just to go there and say to the poor people, 'We know the true God. We are certain. You know nothing. Out with all your error and gods!' That would make people of other races miserable and they would have no ear for what you might want to tell them. It's our duty to pay attention to them, to love them, not to say, 'He's only an African.' There's no such thing as *only* in the sight of God. He will hold us responsible for the trouble we do not take and for all the love which we do not give to others."

"That is what God is going to ask us?"

"Everybody will be asked when they die about what they did."

"Will he ask about the trouble I took?"

"Isabel, think always of the good thief who died near Jesus. He was sorry. He saw Jesus very near him and suddenly he understood God's plan and goodness."

116

"So a person can be bad all his life and then at the end be sorry!"

"Do you think people are going to know if they will have time to be sorry? And if a person is sorry, do you think that he can do this if he has not been sorry in his whole life? Even little girls must be ready to die. That doesn't mean that you've got to be thinking about death all the time. No, it means that you must live rightly for God and with God. Death won't be terrifying then. You know where you are going. And now pray for Uncle Arnim. Pray for a good death."

The man with the knife

Every morning Isabel meets a "man." A prudent attempt to find out the truth. Imaginary creations of children. Signs of a child's sense of sex. How a child can be helped.

"Every morning I meet a man," Isabel announced very importantly one morning at breakfast.

"Well, and . . . ?" broke in Peter.

"Mommy, he won't let me tell you. . . ."

"Oh, Isabel and her man," grumbled her brother.

"Well, then, what does the man want, Isabel? Tell me."

"He tells me stories about a castle where he lives with his children. They do nothing but play. And he has a knife and—and—and a knife, too!"

"Know what, Isabel, we're going into my room and you can tell me the whole story in peace while I do some sewing."

"With a knife, with a knife," chants Peter in a high dramatic soprano.

"Now, then, what about the man with the knife? Do you meet him often?"

"Very often!"

"Every day?"

"Almost every day but not on Wednesday."

"Did you see him yesterday?"

118

"Yes."

"But yesterday was Wednesday. Did he come just the same? Maybe he won't come on Thursday and Sunday?"

"No, he doesn't come on Sunday."

"How long has he been coming now?"

"For three days."

"Then, Monday, Tuesday, Wednesday!"

"Yes, but not on Wednesday."

"How does he look?"

"Pretty gold clothes and a wig and shiny shoes!"

"Doesn't it occur to anyone that he is strangely dressed?"

"Oh, I'm the only one who sees him, Mommy."

"Oh, yes. And can he tell nice stories?"

"He speaks only French. . . ."

"Do you understand him?"

"I can when he talks about the castle. But now he doesn't want to come any more."

"Why?"

"Because I told him you would take his knife away!"

"And he probably didn't like that?"

"No, he didn't, but I told Emmy, too."

"Emmy?"

"Yes, she knows him, too. She's seen him in Augsburg."

"With you?"

"Yes, with me, Mommy. I think with me," she said very hesitatingly, "but I've never been in Augsburg. . . ."

"That makes no difference, Isabel. If he wants to talk to me, call me right away."

"The man has heard everything. He probably won't come any more."

"The man has heard everything? I know. But, you know, if the man isn't wearing gold clothes and he wants to talk to you, run away and don't answer. Come for me."

"Does he want to eat me?"

"No."

"I don't talk to strange men."

"No, you don't talk with them."

"Even if they are nice, Mommy?"

"Even then not."

The result of this talk was that Isabel turned down an offer by our town policeman who wanted to give her a ride. The story about the man with the gold clothes and knife was pure fantasy. A gruff answer, a brutal revelation for the sake of truth, would have brought Isabel into real need. As it was, she unmasked a story of her own making until less and less of it remained.

But why did she make these stories up? Probably she did this to get even with her brothers who likewise had interesting things to tell, or this might also be the way all little girls *make up* stories about a man with a knife. It reveals an awakening sense of sex. Indignation would not have helped. On the contrary, it would have done harm, just as irony would have. How easy it is for us to be ironic with children, but it renders children powerless and rigid while at the same time humiliating them. How powerless they are in the face of it and how demeaned.

Even such phantastic imaginings ought to be taken seriously because they reflect some insurmountable problem for the child. We want to help them, indeed, and we want to continue helping them.

St. Joseph is always cooking gruel

In the mountains. Nature, an experience for the child. I lift up my eyes to the mountains. What is a psalm? A child can pray the psalms. Jesus prayed the psalms. My God, my God, why have you forsaken me? Who was David? Why is my name David? The Holy Innocents. Let the little ones come to me. Little children and holy communion. St. Joseph, a relative of David's. Was Joseph an old man? How old was Mary? Why did Joseph want to send Mary away? And the angel declared unto Mary. What did Mary answer? Joseph loved Mary. Joseph, patron of all families.

WE have been ten days in an abandoned and charming part of the Alps where there are only a few scattered huts. The little one we borrowed from friends is situated more than a mile up and it is close to a small forest which overlooks a frozen lake. It is surrounded by mighty peaks, five thousanders. Every day we have the sun and a radiant blue sky.

David looks like a nut with bright eyes, or perhaps, like an overripe apricot! On one of our walks we stop suddenly before a tremendously big mountain and look up at it. David says, "This is the way Moses looked at the Mount of Sinai!"

"I lift up my eyes to the mountains from whence help comes. My help is from the Lord who made heaven and earth.

"That is a psalm, David, a song of God, a prayer which was once sung by the great King David before the old King Saul."

"But that was the little David in the big Goliath story . . . !"

"Yes, but when he sang these songs of God he used to sit near the aging Saul who listened."

"And David also played on the harp."

"David, every Mass begins with a psalm. We can also pray the psalms even if we are small."

He who watches over you neither slumbers nor sleeps. No, the protector of Israel does not sleep.

He is the shade over your right hand so that the sun will not scorch you by day nor the moon molest you by night.

May the Lord protect you from all evil.

"You have often read that to us before but now I really understand what it means."

"When Jesus was hanging on the cross in an agony of death he prayed one of the psalms of David: 'My God, my God, why have you forsaken me?' He probably said the rest quietly to himself."

"I always thought that Jesus cried out . . ."

"He prayed one of the psalms of David."

"Why is my name David? Do you like the psalms so well that you're always thinking that they come from David?"

"Yes, I have a special love for the psalms and King David is certainly very close to me, and St. Joseph was of the family of David. I named you David in remembrance of the great King

David. You are named also in memory of the many dead Jewish children who died somewhere in Germany, Poland, and France. Nobody ever calls their names anymore. I've told you that so often already. But exactly because we know Christ and love him let us build a bridge to these dead. And when I call David through the garden, I sometimes think about them. In your name they are still alive."

"Probably one of the children on the lap of Jesus was also called David!"

"He put his arms around them and that made their mothers very happy."

"But the disciples didn't like it because they didn't want Jesus to do that, Mommy!"

"They just wanted to protect Jesus from the crowd of people which was forever wanting something from him. They were not bad."

"I thought they didn't like children."

"Of course they liked children. When Jesus was no longer with them they must surely have cured children and above all they baptized them. They certainly did think of children, David."

"But King David didn't know Jesus?"

"No."

"That's too bad. He would have been so happy and then there would have been more psalms. Did St. Joseph sing psalms?"

"I think so, yes!"

"He was related to King David, too. And it was hard also for St. Joseph to walk to Bethlehem?"

"Had a hard time to walk, you mean?" I asked cautiously because I wanted very much to find out what was behind the question.

"He was so old, as old as Grandfather with the cane. He must have had to lean on a cane. And he didn't have any teeth!"

"No teeth?"

"He was always cooking gruel not only for the baby Jesus but also because he couldn't bite. I've seen it in a picture in a book!"

"But, David, Jesus' father, Joseph, was not old at all. He was a young strong man, a carpenter, who wanted to be engaged to a young girl as old as Gabrielle, about fourteen. He was a lovely young bridegroom. Now picture to yourself how he felt when he discovered that his bride was expecting a little baby. . . ."

"But she wasn't married!"

"That's just it. And so that was bad and Joseph was sad. . . ."

"Didn't he want her any more?"

"No, he didn't seem to want her. But he loved her just the same. And instead of being angry and telling all around what a bad bride he had, he simply wanted to send her back home quietly. But an angel came to him during the night and said to him, 'Keep Mary and love her. Protect her and the child. Her child is the child of God, a child of the Holy Spirit!'"

"The mother of God had her baby Jesus in another way? Not like Papa and you?"

"No, the angel came to her and said, 'Mary, there is no other Mary like you. God picked you out from all the other women and he loves you especially. You will have a child by the Holy Spirit.'"

"Just like that?"

"Just like that. But, you know, Mary asked, 'How is this going to be? I'm still a young girl. I'm not married. I've never lived with a man like a man and wife do. Can I really expect a child?' 'Yes,' the angel answered. 'God wants it to be like this. The Holy Spirit will come over you and you will bring a son into the world!' "

"A son is a baby, isn't it, Mommy?"

"Naturally. —'And you must call him Jesus.' "

"And when the angel says something like that to a pure beautiful girl like Mary, it must be right. And Mary answered, 'I'll obey. I'm a servant of the Lord.' Everything that God said to her she will do and obey. And Joseph understood. He kept her and cared for her and the child."

"Later did they have other children?"

"No. St. Joseph understood that Mary was especially holy because she had carried Jesus in her body.

"Indeed, he loved Mary just as much as Papa and Mommy love each other, but not as husband and wife who want children. —'We want to live together and to love each other and to live for Jesus,' they said. Joseph could most certainly have had children, but he made a sacrifice. He cared for Mary and Jesus. He was good and tender with them. He loved Jesus as if he were his own child.

"His whole life was very humble, so much so that we know very little about him, even when we read the Bible. And yet we know a lot. We know that he loved God and that he obeyed him just as soon as God demanded it of him. He's the patron saint of every family. That's why we pray to him every day, 'St. Joseph, protect us all. You know what worries we can have. You certainly remember the time you looked for Jesus in the temple. Help me. Amen.' "

126

I think about the transports carrying the Jewish children

The dead Jewish children. Terrible crimes against children of the world. Suffering of the children in Africa, India, Hiroshima. Prayer for Daniel.

TOMORROW the Pax Christi Movement celebrates the memory of the many Jewish children who died in concentration camps. I can't say how much I wish we could all mourn these children as if they had been our own. *I* am the Jewish mother. *I* share the sorrow of many other Jewish mothers. *My* child was torn away from me and killed. *My* child had to ride on a strange truck with many other children bound for death in a concentration camp, —a place where terrible things awaited them, hunger, thirst, illness, abandonment, solitude, insecurity, brutality, murder, sadism, the cruelest, most horrible cheerlessness. It saddens me to recall it. Do you understand, Isabel, how I feel when I stand sometimes by Daniel's bed? Horror and despair seize me and I think of the parents who had to look on while their children were dragged off. They never saw them again, and today, even today, these parents have to go on living without their children.

I stood this evening at Daniel's bed as he slept and I covered him. He really was not too uncovered, but I had the feeling that my tenderness and concern were forcing me to tuck the

127

blankets a bit closer to his little body. How contentedly he lay there, watched over, happy and secure in a rhythmic pattern of a carefree life. And as I stroked him gently with my hand, my thoughts travelled back to the Polish children who were herded together during the war. The memory causes me real pain.

The oldest of these children was ten or twelve, the youngest two. Filthy and worn out, they roamed around like wolves combing the woods for food. At night they crawled together like animals into any place they could find in order to be able to sleep. Or, I see Daniel, crying, cold, dirty, pale, dragged along by his brothers and sister, without warmth, cruelly treated, forlorn. I think about the transports of Jewish children. Four thousand they were from France, the oldest thirteen, the youngest from one and a half to two years of age. They were on trucks, hunted out from everywhere, without food, loaded, unloaded. At first the older ones protected the smaller ones, but after a while, weary and exhausted themselves, they looked on with indifference as the smaller ones died.

I think about the fearfully thin Negro boy from the Congo. He is about six years old and he crouches near his mother who lies on the ground unable to continue further because she is only skin and bones. I see before me a little Indian girl holding in her arms a baby who is crying frightfully from hunger. The little mother has become apathetic from the sorrow which she can no longer bear.

O Daniel, how close this all is, and who knows if you will always be sheltered, or if I shall one day be going around in the street, not knowing where I am going, wailing like the Jewish mother in the ghetto of Warsaw pictured in the documentary film *Mein Kampf*. With her dead child in her arms, someone about your age, she runs and screams and screams and not one of the passers-by pays any attention to her. The dead lie naked in the street and no one cares about them.

Or, will you have to dance in a concentration camp as did the poor little five-year-olds who, with a terrible grin on their face, made an attempt at dancing in the hope that the audience would give them money for food? Sometimes when I see you laughing happily, my children, the little Jewish child with what was left of his human smile so unlike a child, so old, suddenly appears among you.

You could have been that little child whom I saw in the film on Hiroshima after the explosion of the atom bomb. He was standing in a large wasteland with hundreds of other children. He was burnt. He had no skin and he leaped unceasingly with excruciating pain shrieking piercingly so that I cannot forget it. I can still hear his voice in the stillness of the night. How can a world in which there are so many mothers who have borne children endure this thorn in its flesh? How can it bear the thought of little children who have suffered so much and may suffer again? What sort of humanity is it where so much can be waiting for you, my darling, my little darling sleeping so peacefully in a warm clean bed? You could be tomorrow like the little Arab who was arrested because he was carrying documents. You could be tortured into finally talking and betraying where your own people were hiding.

My Daniel who can say only *mama* to me now, my little late-talker, my silent darling already understanding so much, the day may come when you who are spared so many efforts at talking now may be forced to talk. You have not said *no* yet but only a loving *yes*.

129

God protect you, my treasure, my heart, my child.

May God strengthen you, my dear little son.

May God stand by you if ever this should happen to you.

God grant that by that time you will know so much about him that you will be true to him.

My Daniel, sleep, sleep, my darling.

Peter's parents take their lives

Both parents commit suicide. Sensation. Children do not always realize the horror of such an act. Why is there suicide? A sickened spirit. Suicide, a serious sin. Judas Iscariot. Self-righteousness. Bless yourself in the presence of a dead person. The story of the savings bank. I don't want to be punished alone. I was treated unfairly. I want to get even. The brothers help. The story of the glowing sword. Conscience.

"Mommy, a child came to school today and said that Peter Miller's mother and father had killed themselves."

"Who killed whom, Manuel? Aren't those robber stories which children often tell?"

"No, Mommy, really not. His father lay down on the railroad tracks and waited until the train came and his mother put a rope around her neck and it had something to do with the door handle. I'm not so sure just what but she's dead, too." Manuel relayed this story with self-assurance and eagerness.

It renders me speechless and shocks me partly because of the frightful tragedy and partly because of the fact that Manuel was so casual about it. It was just a gruesome irrelevant story for him.

"And Peter," I ask softly, "what has become of the poor child?"

"He was brought to Berlin by his uncle."

131

"Does this sound all right to you—just a little trip with the uncle without father and mother?"

"How come?" Manuel asks astonished.

"Peter's mother is dead and she can't ever again take her little boy in her arms when he cries or falls down. She'll never be able to pray with him in the evening or be around to fix his clothes. Nobody will know what Peter's favorite dish is."

"Yes, but why? Is she really dead?"

"You told me the story yourself!"

"When?"

"Just now, darling!"

"Is Peter's father dead, too?"

"If a train ran over him, can he still be alive . . . ?"

"Just the same as if I crush an ant with my foot," says Manuel shaken. "I had no idea that his parents were dead."

He stands there quite desperate.

"It's terrible that Peter is an orphan and has to go away. But it will be much worse when he finds out what happened to his parents."

"He knows already. Jerry Menz has already told him."

"I think that was awful. Why do you suppose he did that?"

"Because he thought it was a nice story."

"No, because now I know they're dead."

"You know, Manuel, Peter's mother was very sick. She didn't know what she was doing. Life is a gift from God. No one can decide when he wants to put an end to it."

"But if someone is so sick and has so much pain, can he?"

"No, not even then, because we don't know the ways and purposes of God."

"What are his purposes?"

"God's plans for us, his will."

"And what happened to Peter's father?"

"Maybe he was sick, too. Maybe he didn't know what to do either so he just lay down on the tracks."

"But we're not supposed to do that."

"That's right. We're not, and suicide is a serious sin, perhaps the worst. There is no way of setting the matter right again. But we may not judge these people. We'll never know what ever could have happened to them that made everything so dark inside them."

"But, Mommy, they just completely forgot Peter!"

"We don't know that either."

"They were bad. They ought to be dead."

"No, they were not bad. We didn't know them and we don't know how poor and utterly alone they might have been. We have no right to say anything against them. We can only pray for them."

"Judas was a murderer, too. . . ."

"After he betrayed the Saviour he became aware of the fact that he had done something terrible."

"But he was sorry and that's why he brought the money back."

"Yes, that's why. But then instead of continuing to be sorry, he despaired so much that he could no longer think, 'I have handed an innocent person to death. I have betrayed Jesus and it all happened through my own fault.' In order to put an end to these painful thoughts he hanged himself and died."

"But he wasn't sick, Mommy, and he knew it."

"Yes, he did know what he was doing. This evening you must say this prayer for Peter's parents: Eternal rest grant to them, O Lord, and let perpetual light shine upon them."

"And when I meet the hearse on the street I must bless myself."

"We should always do this remembering to pray for the dead."

"Supposing it's an auto?"

"Then, too."

"It goes so fast . . . !"

"But you can always pray: Lord, let him rest in peace."

"Mommy, are you going to live a long time?"

"I would like to on account of you, but we cannot be sure."

"You're always saying that we can't be sure."

"Of course. I'm sure that I love you, you foolish little boy!"

At this point Isabel stormed furiously into my room.

"Mommy, Manuel's bank was empty and he took money from my bank."

"Did he ask you?"

"No, he did it without saying a word."

The following developed! We had let a friend of ours and his three children have our house while we were on vacation. The little ones had broken into the bank and had probably squandered its contents. Manuel, who is very thrifty, was so shaken by this that he looked around for a rather unusual solution. He took Isabel's bank and simply divided the contents between his bank and hers.

I took him into my room to talk with him.

"I can't help it. It's not my fault. I didn't do it."

And he kept repeating this like a refrain: "I can't help it. It's not my fault. Why should I be punished for something I didn't do? Isabel should be punished, too!"

"But she didn't do it either."

"I don't want to be punished."

I wasn't getting anywhere. He had become very stubborn and bitter.

"You took something which didn't belong to you."

"But something was taken from me. Everything was taken!"

"But you did the same thing to Isabel that was done to you. You'll have to give Isabel her money back."

"No, I won't give it back to her! I can't help it. It's not my fault."

"If you had at least asked beforehand!"

"She would have said no," he interrupted.

"You have broken the seventh commandment. You shall not take what does not belong to you."

"First the one who stole from me has to be punished and then I'll go and give her the money back."

"No, you'll have to bring that money back whether you know or don't know if you'll get your own money back. Someone did something wrong to you and now you want to take revenge by doing the very same thing to someone else."

Gradually he became less and less sure of himself. He went to his bank, took some money out, and threw it at Isabel's feet.

"You others leave, please," I said.

"Manuel, come here. Pick the money up, please. How are you going to be able to sit at table with this resentment in your heart, this anger against Isabel who is really innocent? How are you going to be able to serve at God's altar this evening when you're so angry? Go and put the money back into Isabel's bank. Then we can discuss the matter further."

He obeyed. I asked Isabel to thank him and to let the matter drop.

After the prayers in the evening the brothers said, "We want to give Manuel some money and Isabel, too."

Manuel was completely astonished at such generosity. But Peter wanted no part of sentimentality. He merely said, "Take it now and let's hear no more!"

But the story took an unexpected turn. I received a letter. It contained the following: "Dear Mrs. Becker, There is some money in a blue dish in your writing desk. When Bettina was playing with the money bank some of the money rolled out. I forgot to mention it to you in our haste." So Manuel got his money back and what his brothers had given to him was returned to them. On Sunday each one gave a little more in the offertory collection.

"Isabel, I'm sorry. I understand now."

"He understands because he's got everything back again!" Peter chimed in.

"That wasn't right, Peter. You shouldn't think such things about your brother."

"I'd like to tell you another story which a White Father from Africa told me. There lived a missionary near a large river on the

Ivory Coast. He took care of the Negroes who lived nearby. He brought them medicines and food. Once a month he rode down the river to the coast in his pirogue, that is, his little canoe, and this was his way of getting medicine for the sick. One day the little boat was missing. The missionary went to the chief and said, 'I can't get to the harbor without my little boat and you'll be without medicine. Now see to it that I have my boat back.' The chief assembled his tribal leaders and asked them who had taken the boat. No one answered. Then the chief took a sword, built a fire, and put the sword into the flames. When it was glowing he took it out and let it cool completely. Then he commanded his seven leaders to line up in a row and to put out the left foot. He went to each and touched his foot with the cold sword. The fifth man cried out loud. There was a large burn on his foot. 'Get the boat,' the chief said quietly. The man vanished only to reappear on the river with the boat which he had hidden."

The children were speechless.

"That's magic," Manuel said.

"No, that's fear," Peter commented.

"It's deserved punishment," Andrew put in.

Very often children are intolerably severe towards the mistakes of others.

"That was his conscience," Isabel said. "That's why the cold sword burned him."

"Once when I was small," Peter related, "I took a sausage in the dining room. You looked for it but I didn't say anything. Later I fell down the steps in the garden and I spit it up. But still I didn't say anything."

I see that Peter understood the story of the sword.

Did the apostles also anoint with oil?

An accident. The anointing with oil, —a sacrament. How does one prepare for the last anointing? Why salt? Confession before the anointing. The praying of the family. The sacred act. The blessing of the Holy Father through the parish priest. The first anointing of the sick. Why oil? The strengthening.

"D ID the bell ring last night, Mommy?" asked Andrew.

"Yes, it was Mrs. Ludwig who came after me. Her husband had had an accident with his car and he was carried home because it happened almost in front of the house."

"Did he die?"

"No, but he's very close to death."

"What did you do?"

"I called the doctor and then went for the priest."

"Did you see right away that it was serious?"

"It was evident and I thought it best to have him anointed."

"Even if he doesn't die?"

"Even if he doesn't die."

"And if he doesn't die he can't be anointed again."

"Of course he can. A person can be anointed many times. The last anointing is supposed to make the sick person stronger. It's supposed to help him and, above all, it frees him from his sins."

"I took our two candlesticks along, some cotton, holy water, a little dish and a cross."

"Why did you take all those things with you?"

"Because I didn't know what the Ludwigs had."

"But if they called the priest . . . ?"

"That doesn't mean that they have everything they need, although it would certainly be nice if they did. We should always have in the house the things we are going to need when the priest comes."

"Maybe they didn't know."

"I covered the table quickly with a white cloth, placed the candlesticks on it, and in the middle I stood the cross. I put some holy water in a little dish and placed a little sprig near it. Then I made six little balls of cotton, filled a glass with ordinary water, placed a spoon near the glass and a small dish with a little salt."

"Salt?"

"Yes, the priest needs salt or bread crumbs in order to purify his fingers after he has used the holy oil. Then I went for the priest."

"Is Mr. Ludwig still unconscious? Can he talk?" asked my little son.

"No, he can't talk, but by looking at him one can see that he understands what is being said. I think he's very much afraid. There was anxiety in his eyes.

"When we got there, Mrs. Ludwig lit the candles. She was crying. The sons of the sick man and his old mother were standing around the bed. She was the only one who was praying with the dying man. He looked at her steadily. The priest took holy water and sprinkled the sick man and all the people in the room. Then he asked us to leave because the sick man might want to go to confession. When we were allowed to return to the room, the priest was reading the story of the centurion of Capharnaum: 'I am not worthy, Lord, that you should come under my roof, but say only the word and my servant will be healed.'

"Then I saw Mr. Ludwig bowing his head twice, very slowly. We all knelt down and with trembling voice I repeated the prayers for the sick. Everyone answered the prayers. The priest took the oil and anointed Mr. Ludwig. He rubbed oil on his eyelids, ears, nose, hands, and feet while he asked God to forgive Mr. Ludwig for the sins he had committed with his eyes, ears, and senses. Each time the priest took a piece of cotton and wiped the place which had been anointed. Then he prayed with us for the sick man who had closed his eyes. Mr. Ludwig now received the sacred host which the priest had brought in his breast-coat pocket. The priest placed the host in the sick man's partially opened mouth. Mr. Ludwig raised his eyes once again. 'Receive the body of Christ, my brother. He will shield you from the evil one and will lead you into eternal life. My brother, give your pain to our Lord Jesus Christ. Be sorry for your sins again and entrust yourself to the will of God.'

"With these words the priest imparted the apostolic blessing on him for the forgiveness of all his sins."

"Can he do that?"

"Of course. He's God's anointed priest."

"For always?"

"For always, come what may."

"Did the apostles *oil* the sick?"

"*Anoint,* we say. St. James must have received this commission from our Lord Jesus himself. Therefore he writes in a letter what a priest should do for the sick."

"Why oil, Mommy?"

"After your bath I rub you with oil to make you strong. They do that to fighters so that their arms and legs can be strong. The anointing of the sick has the same significance."

"When people are anointed they always get better, don't they?"

"Not always, but the sick can be relieved and fortified. The most important part is the forgiveness of sins before one steps into the presence of God."

"But Mr. Ludwig didn't know what was going on!"

"We can't say that. Perhaps he could hear everything and his heart was full of faith. How can we know anything about that, and shouldn't we have done everything in order to strengthen and give him joy? How often does it happen that many sick people look happier in death than they did in life?"

"And then?"

"And then I went back home."

"Do you think that he'll live?"

"No. But we don't know what God has in his mind."

Mr. Ludwig died during the night.

Did Jesus really play when he was small?

Did Jesus laugh? Jesus, a human being. Mary, spotless mother of God. Marriage at Cana. Woman, what is that to you and me? Jesus in the temple. Mommy, you had to look for us once. Did Jesus always obey? How would you like a pilgrimage to the days of Jesus? Didn't you know that I had to be about my Father's business? The obedient Mary. Abraham again. Life as a nomad. Abraham leaves the land of Ur in answer to God's call. God's choice of his people. Abraham and Lot go to Canaan and separate. Abraham goes to the aid of Lot. Abraham, your descendants will be as numerous as the stars of heaven. Abraham, Sarah, and Isaac. God's alliance with Abraham. Abraham's obedience.

"Mommy," says David, "I've never seen a picture of Jesus where he was laughing. Do you suppose he ever laughed?"

"But David, I'm sure that he did laugh. For example, as a baby in the crib he laughed with his mother and father. He laughed when he played with the children of the neighborhood."

"Do you really think he played?"

"Of course I do. He was a child just like any other child while he was at the same time the Son of God. It pleased God the Father to let a young girl come into the world whose soul was clear and transparent. This maiden became the mother of Jesus."

"Was her soul like pretty glass?"

"Yes, without the darkness which Adam and Eve experienced. Mary was without the shadow of sin, immaculate, that is. You know, we sing: 'Hail Mary, tender . . .' She was young and tender, lively and bright. This young fifteen-year-old maiden was very happy about her child. She played with him the way I do with you. She laughed and Jesus laughed back at her."

"What about the wedding at Cana?"

"I'm sure that Mary and Jesus were very happy at the wedding and that they didn't sit gloomy and sad. People can be happy and glad without being hilarious about it. Grandmother often laughs but she doesn't do it out loud. . . ."

"But Jesus was a little grumpy before the miracle at the wedding! He was so mean to his mother, Mommy."

"No, David. I don't think he was. We don't know anything about the expression on his face when he spoke to his mother. It's only an unusual way of saying something."

"But Mary must have felt bad."

"But she must have understood his answer. 'Woman, what is that to you and me? Woman,' Jesus says, 'everything is a mystery between my heavenly Father and me.'* She knew his power. It was very clear to her that Jesus was going to help. What do we know about what Mary had experienced in daily life during Jesus' childhood and youth? Some hidden miracle? Mary certainly knew a great deal. Shall I read to you again about Jesus in the temple?"

"Yes, please."

"All right, then."

* By means of this first miracle Jesus showed for the first time that he was the Son of God. This miracle separates him from his family. He went his own way alone. No one else could travel this road.

David said, rather perplexedly, "But it wasn't very nice of Jesus to go away and let his mother look for him like that. You had to look for me in the summertime when I was at the pond and you didn't know it. And you had told me not to go there!"

That was right. Once I looked for him and his two older brothers in fearful anguish because they delayed an hour and a half coming home in the evening. And as I was searching the neighboring hill, blind with tears, I saw them coming along in the setting sun, their arms full of flowers. I ran towards them and asked, "How could you do that to me? I've looked everywhere for you and I was so worried." They saw my tears and puzzled expression as I stood before their disarming happiness. "But we picked you a lot of flowers, Mommy. They're all for you!"

"Was Jesus like me, not too obedient?" continued David.

"No, darling, he was different. A twelve-year-old Jewish boy belonged to the older people. He was grown up. He had to fast. He had to go to Jerusalem to offer sacrifice. He had to obey the law of Moses just as you'll have to obey the law when you're seven years old. Then you'll have to go to confession. You won't be allowed to eat meat on Friday. You'll have to go to Mass on Sunday and do everything I have to do. . . . When Jesus was twelve he was obliged to go to the temple just like all the other twelve year olds. How he must have looked forward to this! How happy he must have been when the day finally arrived! How often he must have said even when he was only nine, 'Mommy, take me with you. I'm really big enough. Mommy, please, this year!' And still she didn't take him. 'When you're twelve you'll go. The trip is too long.' You know, David, it was more than fifty miles away, maybe even seventy-five. Think how far that is. And they went by foot. A great many people went to Jerusalem coming from everywhere by the thousands. Finally the day came when Jesus was allowed to go. Indeed, almost everyone in Nazareth was going to Jerusalem.

"It was a real pilgrimage. The people sang and prayed the psalms and talked together."

"Just like we do!"

"Jesus was allowed to take part. During the day he walked nearly twenty miles. He was so full of expectation that he must have laughed. He was so grateful to be going along. Jesus was obedient, but as a twelve-year-old boy he was independent. For the first time he was going to the temple of his heavenly Father. Mary knew that Jesus was the Son of God, but while the three were living together in Nazareth they were just as happy as any other family. Mary kept her knowledge deep in her heart. Now Jesus' words must have come to her unmistakably clear. Yes, she knew. 'Didn't you know that I must be about my Father's business? I'm on the earth with you, dear parents, to do the will of my Father always and everywhere.' Mary knew, 'My Jesus is the Son of God. Whatever happens is the will of God. I am living with the Son of God. I take care of him, cook for him just as any mother does for her child. He belongs to God entirely. God's will must be my will.' "

"Like Abraham, Mommy!"

In the meantime Andrew and Peter had come in.

"Now, look, I've been wanting to show you where Abraham lived. Do you see these two rivers? They are the Tigris and

Euphrates, and do you see the land in between? It's a wonderfully rich country because these rivers water it. For thousands of years powerful kings have lived here and Babylon, the capital, had the most beautiful palaces standing in the middle of enchanted gardens. Do you see the cities of Ur and Erech and Lagash right close to Babylon? Abraham lived in Ur with his father Terah, a Semite. Does the word *Semite* remind you of something familiar?"

"It makes me think of Shem, Ham, and Japheth."

"That's right. Shem was Noah's son. He belonged to his tribe. Terah emigrated from the land of Ur with his great herds. He belonged to this tribe. It was common in those days for people to pack up what they owned on camels and donkeys, take wives and children, and wander from place to place. Terah believed in a moon god, honoring him and offering him sacrifice. That was the religion of his forefathers. They had pitched tent in Haran and here Terah died. God called Abraham then: 'Abraham, come out of this land. Take your family and herds with you. I myself will lead you. I don't want you to live among unbelievers. I want to make your tribe a great people. You shall be blessed. I shall accompany you and protect you.' This special word of God is the most important thing."

"Why did God pick Abraham out? Was he especially nice?"

"God does what he wants. He chooses the people he wants to choose. We can never question why because we know so little. He said to Abraham, 'You shall be blessed.' From now on Abraham had to bow to the will of God."

"Wasn't that hard, Mommy?"

"It's always hard but wonderful when God chooses a person

147

and gives him a special work to do. —'Yes, Lord, I will obey.' With that he left for Canaan with his wife Sarah, his nephew Lot, and some herds. Why they should have to go there, Abraham didn't know. But he trusted God and let him guide him. It was very far to Canaan. It had already been more than five hundred miles to Haran. How often they must have been tired and how long it must have all taken! Abraham stopped to rest, pitched tent, took it down again. He kept going towards the south. Take a look at the way they went on this map. It seemed the trip would never end. Abraham was a courteous, peaceable man. His herds and the herds of his nephew Lot had multiplied.

"Quarrels often broke out between the herdsmen of both families."

"Why did they quarrel?"

"Whenever they discovered a well each wanted to be the first to water his cattle."

"Oh, now I understand better."

"Or, if they found a pasture, the herdsmen of Lot envied the herdsmen of Abraham. Now Abraham didn't want this quarrelling so he said to Lot, 'Choose wherever you want to go, Lot, whether it be to the right or to the left.' He, the older of the two, asks the younger about his wishes!"

"But that was smart because then there would be nothing else to say. That's what Peter does sometimes to us!"

"But that wasn't the reason. Abraham really wanted peace, and besides, he was a humble man and he knew how terribly family quarrels upset everyone."

"Like when we quarrel in front of Rudy and say ugly words."

"I think that's so terrible and dishonorable. Mrs. Meinecke

does it often. She scolds her husband when he eats too much or says something wrong."

"When she does that, I feel very embarrassed. I don't know why, but I don't like it."

"So Lot decided to come here where the Dead Sea is. He chose the beautiful Jordan Plain and settled down in Sodom. Abraham continued on to Hebron near the present-day Jerusalem on the way to Bethlehem. And God said to Abraham when Lot had gone, 'All the land which you see will I give to you and to your descendants. They will be as numerous as the sands of the earth.' Then Abraham built an altar to God. Things didn't go too well for Lot, however. Foreign kings occupied the land and they carried him off with everything he owned. Abraham didn't hesitate for a moment. He hurried to the rescue of Lot. With a small group—his own servants and allied neighbors—he attacked the enemy and won."

"Because God protected him and because he had the blessing of God, didn't he, Mommy?"

"Yes, he brought Lot and all his possessions back. He let those who fought with him have the booty. He didn't want anything for himself. He couldn't bear the thought of getting rich on the property of others."

"But now things are different in war. People take everything away," said Peter.

"No," added Andrew very decidedly. "Food is always needed in a country where a war is going on, but one shouldn't take a watch, or," and he thought sharply, "or books in strange houses."

"Was Abraham very happy now?"

"No. In the meantime Abraham and Sarah had become old and they had no children. God saw Abraham's sorrow and he said, 'Abraham, look up to the heavens. Count the stars if you can. Just so numerous will your descendants be.' This thought keeps reappearing in the song 'Praise the Lord. Praise him together with Abraham's seed.' The seed means the children, the children of the children of the children until we came into the world. . . .

"So, Peter, Abraham was happy and he believed God, although he was already old, almost one hundred years old, and Sarah too. 'I will seal a covenant with you, a friendship. As a sign of this Sarah will have a child. . . .' Sarah was too old to have children, but even so, she had a son."

"She got him from God like the Mother of Jesus had him from God," said Andrew.

"Yes, from God. But still the way Papa and I and other parents have children."

"Now God is good again, almost as good as he was with Adam."

"You're so right, Manuel. God is the friend of Abraham in the new friendship. And we, the children of Abraham, are the friends of God if we believe the way he did. You know, of course, what a genealogy is. Abraham is the first in the genealogy of Jesus because Joseph was the foster father of Jesus. That's a place of honor which he well earned. You know the story of Abraham and what happened when Isaac was born."

"Yes, he almost killed him!"

"Yes, Abraham was ready to offer his son Isaac to God if God wanted to try Abraham. But don't forget. Abraham was courteous, peaceable, patient, and friendly. He had a generous heart and a great understanding. God singled him out and yet Abraham remained humble and very obedient. 'Abraham,' God called. —'Here I am, Lord!' —And when we die and God calls us we must answer the way Abraham did: 'Here I am, Lord.' The heavenly banquet will take place with Isaac and Jacob, it says in the Gospel. Abraham, father of those who believe, pray for us."

Things grown-ups can't
remember too well

What is an illegitimate child? Marriage is a sacrament. What is a sacrament? When you have given birth to a child, you are no longer a girl, you are a woman. What is divorce? What is the state? What is the Church? Peter, the first pope. The betrayal by Peter. The miraculous catch of fish. Peter, do you love me? Pasture my lambs. Lord, I love you. Where are you going, Lord? To Rome to be crucified again. The first Christians of the Church. Our Holy Father, Pope John XXIII. The loneliness and sacrifice of a priest's life.

"MOMMY, what's an illegitimate child? I heard Rose say that one of the neighbors in the town had an illegitimate child. . . ."

"I'll tell you exactly. It's a child with no father . . ."

He broke in. "Oh, just like the Mother of God!"

"No, not like the Mother of God. You didn't let me finish. It's a child who is born when the mother is not married."

"But you can't have a child alone."

"No, this woman lived with a man as if she were married to him and a child came from their union. I don't know why the man didn't marry her unless he's already married."

"But if he's already married he can't love someone else, Mommy."

"He ought not, but he did."

"Could you suddenly love another child and not me any more?"

"Are you serious?"

"No, not really, but if something like that happened in Rose's town!"

"You know, illegitimate means, —outside marriage. —Marriage is a sacrament."

"What's a sacrament?"

"A sacrament is a sacred action instituted by Christ. Jesus instituted the sacrament of marriage. Jesus instituted the sacrament of penance, of holy communion, confirmation, ordination to the holy priesthood, the sacrament of the anointing of the sick, and above all, the sacrament of baptism."

"I counted seven things!"

"There are seven sacraments and marriage is one of them."

"But Mommy, how do you know when you love someone?"

"Oh, you can tell. For example, your wife will say to herself before she is your wife, 'This David would be a good father,' or, 'I like him. He's a good man. I'd like to live with him. He would take care of me. I like him very much. I'd like to make a home with him. I'd like him to be the father of my children.'"

"Would the mother of the illegitimate child like to have a home too?"

"Perhaps. She's certainly not happy. Who'll take care of the child later when she has to work because her child has no father? I feel so sorry for her...."

"Will they punish her?"

"Who?"

"The police or the mayor."

153

"No."

"Will God punish her?"

"We don't know, but we may not look down on her."

"Why do you call Annie Mrs. Rein? She doesn't have a husband either."

"Because she has a child. She and the child would suffer if I said *Miss Rein*. When a woman has a child she is called *Mrs*."

"Mrs. Schultz doesn't have a husband either."

"No, she's divorced. She did have a husband but he doesn't live with her any more."

"Where does he live?"

"In another city. He married again."

"Like the Samaritan woman. She married five times."

"Now, whether she really married, we don't know. But Aunt Bonni is divorced too. Both Uncle and Auntie are divorced. The state divorced them, not the Church."

"What's the state? Is it a man?"

"No, the state is the good ordering of people. To this good order belongs the building of good roads, a good fire department, a good police department, good schools, good customs, good hospitals . . ."

"Prisons, too?" asked Isabel.

"Yes."

"But the Church is a building, too, isn't it Mommy?"

"That too. But the Church is something more. It's a community, something like a great big family. Everyone who believes in Jesus belongs to it, everyone who listens to what the Holy Father and the bishops have to say because of the command of Jesus. All the cardinals, bishops, priests, missionaries, Sisters, and many millions of fathers, mothers, and children are together the Church which Jesus instituted."

"Does that mean catholic?"

"The universal Christian Church is called catholic. Jesus founded this Church when he said to his apostle Peter—Peter means rock, 'A rock is a strong stone and on this rock I will build my church.' The Church began to live with Peter. He was the first pope. He led the Church. He was its first pope."

"But Peter denied the Saviour."

"And still he loved Jesus more than anything else. He was weak just like all people are weak. You love me, too, and you certainly don't want to be up to mischief...."

"But I get into mischief just the same. I do again and again."

"But you do keep trying not to get into trouble again. Peter understood then how quickly a person can betray someone he loves the best. He had said to Jesus, 'Even if everyone betrays you, Lord, I won't.'"

"But he said to the maid, 'I don't know this man.'"

"That's what I mean. Peter learned to have sympathy for people after he had betrayed Jesus. He knew his own weakness and so he understood others. I understand you better, David, when I remember that I was once a little child."

"Grown-ups don't remember very well, do they, Mommy? They always say they wouldn't have done such a thing. They were always so good!"

"But I'm not saying that," I answered, provoked.

"No, you only say, 'If I had done such a thing like that, what my mother would have done to me!'"

I'm defeated.

155

"But Jesus remembered that Peter had betrayed him. One day he was standing on the shore as Peter, John, and some of the other disciples were returning from fishing. They had worked all night without catching anything and they were irritable and tired. They didn't recognize the Master, Jesus. Jesus told them to throw their nets back into the water."

"Why did they do that if they didn't recognize Jesus?"

"Because many times fish can be seen better from the shore where fish swarm. That's why. But when their nets became so full that they were in danger of breaking, John said to Peter, 'It is the Lord.' He recognized him because he loved Jesus so much. Peter jumped into the water and swam to the shore so that he could get to Jesus as quickly as possible.

"There was a coal fire on the shore. The fish could be cooked and there was even bread there! 'Come,' said Jesus, 'let's eat.' And he gave them bread and fish."

"Had Jesus gotten the meal ready?"

"Yes, he fixed the meal just the way a mother would have done for her children. I get much joy when I think of how Jesus lit the fire. He was thinking of how tired his disciples were and he wanted to refresh them. And after the meal Jesus asked Peter, 'Do you love me more than all of these friends who are with us?' 'Yes, Lord,' Peter said. 'You know that I love you.' 'Feed my lambs. Be their shepherd, the shepherd of my flock.' 'Do you love me, Simon, son of John?' 'Yes, Lord,' Peter said again. 'You know that I love you.' 'Feed my lambs,' Then Jesus asked again, 'Simon, son of John, do you love me?' Peter became sad."

"Perhaps he thought Jesus didn't believe him," suggested our Peter, subdued and really sad. But then he cried, "I've another

156

idea. Maybe Jesus was thinking that Peter had denied him three times."

"How wonderful it was for Peter to be able to answer such a question. 'Yes, Lord, I love you,' for his heart was filled with love. 'Feed my lambs. Be their shepherd.' —That shows that Jesus believed him and that he trusted him. 'No one else shall be the leader of my people. You, Peter, will one day die for me.'"

"Did Jesus know ahead of time?"

"Yes, he knew that Peter would die on a cross. Do you know the story they tell in Rome where Peter died when he wanted to run away from the persecutions? He'd already left the city and was hurrying along one of the famous Roman roads which led through the country into the mountains. Our Lord came face to face with him and he was carrying his cross. 'Where are you going, Lord?' Peter asked. 'I'm going to Rome to be crucified again,' Jesus said to him. Peter turned around and went back to Rome where death on a cross was waiting for him. This Peter was the first Holy Father. And all who believed in Jesus and let themselves be baptized became the Church of the Christians.

"Peter guided them, visiting them and teaching them. They learned from him how to bring the message of Jesus to the unbaptized. He gave them through Jesus the power to heal the sick, to baptize, to forgive sins. With the power of the Holy Spirit Peter became a fisher of people and he led them to Jesus. He knew what he should say in order to touch the hearts of the people so that they would want to be baptized. The disciples helped him to carry out his office. They were his priests. They were supposed to represent Jesus who was no longer in this world.

"The Church grew and there were more and more priests and people who were baptized. Today it's just the same."

"But what did the Christians do when Peter died?"

"They chose a new Holy Father who would guide them and his children. When our pastor went to Rome he talked with the Holy Father."

"Did the Pope talk with him?"

"Yes. He said to him, 'When you go back to your church give the people my blessing, especially the children. Take them in your arms and pat them for me as a tender greeting from their Father in Rome. They are the hope of the world. I love all children with all my heart.'"

"That's what I thought, Mommy. Our pastor was different when he came back from Rome."

"The priest prays for us. He talks with Jesus about us. He talks with us about Jesus. That's why he didn't marry and why he lives alone—just to carry out his office to the best of his ability. That's not easy. He would probably like to have children like other men, but the priest has given up a family of his own. Therefore we must be good to priests. We must pray for them."

Why do you ask
when you know I'm lying?

Jesus goes to Jerusalem. Biblical account of the passion. Was Jesus actually afraid? How did Jesus suffer? The Mother of Jesus on the way of the cross. The Mother of Jesus with John under the cross. Andrew still has the light on. Andrew denies. Andrew tells a lie. He confesses. I want to help you tell the truth.

"I'M going to read you something from the Gospel of St. Matthew. But first look at the map of the Holy Land and see how close Bethphage is to Jerusalem.

"Jesus went with his disciples towards Jerusalem. When he approached Bethphage near the Mount of Olives he took two of his disciples to one side and said to them, 'Go into the place which lies there before you. You'll find an untied donkey there and no one has as yet ridden it. Untie it and bring it to me. If anyone should want to know what you are doing, tell them that the Master needs it. He'll give it to you immediately.'

"They went, found the donkey, and untied it. Several people who happened to be standing there said, 'Why are you untying the donkey?' The disciples answered them as Jesus had instructed them to do. So the people let them go. The disciples led the donkey to Jesus and placed their clothing over it as Jesus mounted. Then many people spread their garments on the road while others cut down branches from the trees and strewed them on the ground. The crowds which preceded and followed cried out, 'Hosanna to the son of David. Blessed is he who comes in the name of the Lord. Hosanna in the highest!'"

"That was really like a procession," said Peter. "I'd love to do that on Palm Sunday but it's not allowed any more. I like to shout when I'm happy!"

"But you can sing out loud on Sunday and you can hold your palm very high."

"But we really can't be too happy because we know that Jesus has to die," Andrew commented.

"Yes, but Jesus will rise from the dead, too."

"But first he has to die, Mommy."

"I'm going to read the whole passion story to you. Then you can ask questions." They listened with great attention. When I was reading about the terrible fear which Jesus had in the Garden of Gethsemane, Peter broke in with: "I wondered, Mommy, was Jesus really afraid the way we're afraid? He was the Son of God!"

"Yes, but the Son of God was a human being like you and me. Jesus loved his Father more than anything else and he loved us so much that he offered himself to his Father with all the pain he was suffering in his body and with all the sadness of his soul. —'No one is taking my life away from me. I am giving it,' said Jesus. 'I want to save the people. I want to take all their sins upon me.' So Jesus let himself be crowned with thorns and mocked by people who didn't believe that he was the Son of God. He let people strike him, spit on him, hit him in the face without turning away from them. . . ."

"But that must have hurt very much," persisted Peter. "Can

Jesus suffer more than human beings? Or does he suffer some other way because he is the Son of God?"

"No, Peter, he suffered the same way we do. He was human."

"I'm afraid I couldn't suffer like that," said Peter.

"But lately when you went to the dentist you were very brave . . ."

"But I was awfully afraid, Mommy!"

"But you were very brave just the same. You overcame your fear."

"No, I didn't. I was afraid all the time."

"Yes, but in spite of that, you did hold out. That's the most important thing! —Let's go on.

"Jesus had to carry his cross which was much too heavy for him and a man had to help him with it. Jesus kept falling on the ground. . . ."

"Where was his mother, Mommy?"

"She was standing on the edge of the road and she could see how her son was suffering. That's without doubt the worst part of it, when a mother sees her child in such a pitiful condition and she can't help him. Mary knew, too, that Jesus had to travel this terrible journey. How often had she already said yes to God, 'Yes, I will obey. Do with me whatever you will.' And her heart was broken. She cried, 'O my son Jesus!' She thought about the time she held him in her arms when he was small. How gladly she would have forced her way through the crowd to him and support him, but she had to remain silent and still. Finally Jesus was nailed to the cross. His mother stood beneath it. She had followed him with John, Jesus' great friend, and a few weeping women. Jesus sees his mother and speaks to her in spite of his pain, 'That is now your son.' He meant John and he said to him, 'She is now your mother, John.' And from then on Mary lived at John's house."

"Where was St. Joseph all the time?"

"It doesn't say. He must have died. Otherwise, he would have been standing beneath the cross and Mary would have gone back to live with him. Who could have given her more comfort? Then with a great cry Jesus died on the cross."

"That's why we kiss the feet of Jesus on Good Friday. I always do this well. I like to kiss his feet because I'm always so terribly sorry for the way Jesus died," said Peter.

"And tomorrow I'll tell you about Easter!"

On this evening I had to give another talk and could only get back home at ten o'clock. The light was still burning in Andrew's room, as I could see from the garden.

When I came into his room he was lying there with eyes wide open but the light was out.

"Aren't you asleep yet, Andrew?"

"Yes, I'm already sleeping."

"Then why did you just put your light out? Were you reading?"

"I didn't have the light on."

"But I saw it from the garden. And besides, the light was still warm when I put it on just now."

"I didn't have the light."

"But Andrew, that is stark nonsense. I know that you had your light on and you keep insisting that you didn't. One of us must be foolish. I'm not scolding. I just want you to tell me the truth."

"I am telling the truth."

Things got worse and worse. I insisted. All of a sudden Andrew seemed to be an evil opponent whom I wanted to attack and force into a humble admission, "Yes, I'm lying."

Suddenly he cried out agonizingly, "Then why do you keep asking me when you can see that I am lying?"

My vindictiveness and hardness fell from me like old rags. I took him in my arms. "My poor darling, don't harden yourself like that. You're quite right. Why did I keep asking you in such a painful way?"

"Mommy, I was reading because I just simply wanted time for once to read as much as I wanted to."

"Yes, I understand."

"But when you asked so suddenly I could only say no. And because I said no I was too proud not to keep saying no. I'm sorry. I had the light on."

He cried. He sat there in his bed, very small, pale, and unhappy, his little shoulders heaving helplessly under his thin night clothes.

"I want to make a suggestion to you, Andrew. Every Saturday you may read until a quarter past nine. And no one will disturb you. We just want to make sure of one thing, —try to tell the truth, or else just tell me, 'Mommy, I can't say now.' A lie involves so much. One lie leads to another and things become more and more complicated. Try to speak the truth in the very smallest things. Tell the truth to yourself."

"You know, Mommy, at the end I was almost sure that I didn't have the light on."

"That's the temptation, the temptation of the evil spirit. After

163

that, people can't live right any more because they become stifled. You've seen for yourself."

He kissed me very lovingly. Half an hour later he was fast asleep.

That God can eat

Why did Jesus wash the feet of his apostles? Jewish customs. Peter refuses. Should we wash the feet of others? We are supposed to help. Suffering people. Self-justification. Generous help. Goodness and mercy. Helping a poor person is not too easy. Selflessness. Why does Jesus want to eat with the apostles? The meal. The Passover meal. The bitter herbs and unleavened bread. In memory of the exodus from Egypt. The new paschal meal with Jesus. Take and eat, this is my body. I am the living bread. Offense at the customs of the Jews. Will you also go away? We are remaining with you, Lord. Your blood which was poured out for many. We are the many. Did Judas eat the body of Jesus, too?

"Why did Jesus wash the apostles' feet? Were they dirty?"

"That was a custom," Peter explained.

"Even if they were clean, even after a bath, the host washed the feet of his guests. If he was a rich man he employed non-Jewish slaves to wipe their feet afterwards. The most lowly Jew found this humiliating. But Jesus wanted to show the apostles this act of humility. He did it out of love to teach them that no service was too far beneath him which would demonstrate his love for them."

"But Peter didn't want it," my Peter tossed in.

165

"Peter had a passionate heart. He was a little impatient and impetuous."

"Later he cut the servant's ear off!"

"That's why he didn't want his beloved Lord to wash his feet."

"Now I understand Mary Magdalen when she washed the feet of Jesus and wiped them with her hair. She did for Jesus what Jesus did for the apostles," Manuel said.

"Yes, with this difference. She did it for someone she loved, but Jesus did it for all of the apostles."

"Even for Judas?"

"Even for him. —'You are clean, but not all of you,' said Jesus."

"Are we supposed to wash people's feet?"

"No, but we're supposed to do things for others whoever they happen to be. We shouldn't say, 'I'm going to help this person, but I won't help that person because I don't like him.' "

"Am I supposed to sit near Susey Dreher, Mommy? She smells so bad."

"Then forget yourself and think of how she lives at home. What an awful barracks of a home. Think of how she has to get water at the railroad station because they don't have any water at home."

"But they have a television!"

"Yes, they have. There are people who no longer have the strength to lift themselves out of their misery. Then they buy a television set instead of a bathtub."

"But that isn't right," said Manuel sternly.

"You say it's not right. You say that because you're secure. You have a clean home. You're warm. But the Drehers know only the squalor and discomfort of their barracks to which they have accustomed themselves. And when they can't take any more, they turn on the television. I'm not saying it's right, but I am saying that it's not right for you to judge. There are people in Paris who call themselves the Little Brothers of the Poor. They seek out the poor and in the Spring, for example, they bring them the tastiest things which can be found."

"Isn't that expensive?"

"Yes, it's expensive. But they ask why is it that when we give gifts we always say, 'That's good enough for the poor. They are poor. If we don't bring them something they're that much more the worse off.' The Little Brothers, however, say, 'We want to give them the best which will bring them joy. They ought to forget their poverty. Each of these poor people is Christ. And what wouldn't we give to our Lord!'"

"But if we collected all the money, we could build a house and the poor could live in it and have sleeping room to sleep in," said Manuel.

"Would you like to sleep in a sleeping room—always with somebody else?"

"No."

"It's actually not so easy to help the poor," I comment.

"During recess when I give Susey my lunch she takes it and afterwards she sticks her tongue out at me!"

"And what do you do then?"

"Once I stuck out my tongue back at her and another time I chased her so that I could yell at her, 'Do I have to say it? You conceited thing! I give you my lunch and you can't even say thank you! All you can do is stick out your tongue! Wait and see if I give you my lunch again!'"

"Yes," said Isabel, subdued, "it makes me mad. I'd like to be thanked, too. But I understand. I think Susey acts that way

167

because her mother doesn't give her any lunch and because she's so unhappy."

"If someone is unhappy, he gets cross. Then he can hold out better," said Peter.

"Susey can't stand your pity. That's why she behaves the way she does. I suggest you give your lunch to the teacher and she'll give it to Susey without telling her where it came from."

"But it's not so nice as if we did it ourselves," murmured my disappointed child.

"But then you're really doing something for Susey."

"It's always so strange to think that God can eat," said Andrew.

"I've wanted so very much to eat this Pasch with you. —Is that what you mean, Andrew?" Jesus wanted to celebrate the paschal meal once again with his apostles. Why do you think I'm so happy when you take an early bus home at noon?"

"So that we can all be together at the table."

"If we have to wait until two o'clock and then eat alone, things don't taste so good to me and I eat like a hog! Sometimes I've even put my feet up on another chair and put the dish in my lap. I read, too, because I get so bored," said Peter.

"It does make sense to sit together at table. We see one another, eat together, pass the food to one another, and share what's left!"

"Yes, it does make sense!"

"That's just exactly what Jesus felt. The paschal meal of the Jews, the Easter meal, was a magnificent celebration. The people prayed during the meal, ate, sang, and drank. They all had to have a piece of the lamb. They all had to drink some of the wine and eat some unleavened bread and bitter herbs. These bitter herbs were eaten in remembrance of the exodus from Egypt. Moses had led the Jews from Egypt because the Egyptians had treated the Jews so badly that they couldn't live there any longer."

"But why did they eat unleavened bread, Mommy?"

"Because the Jews had to leave Egypt so quickly that they didn't have the time to wait for raised bread."

"What's the paschal feast?"

"When the Jews wanted to leave Egypt, Pharaoh, the king, wouldn't let them go. So God sent the Egyptians a plague and the child who was born first in each Egyptian family died. Andrew was the first one born in our family.

"Now God had told the Jews beforehand that they were to sprinkle their doorposts with the blood of the lamb, and then when the angel of death came in the night, he went into the houses of the Egyptians and took their first-born child. But he went by the houses which had blood from the lamb sprinkled on the doorposts. Passover means going over. That's why the feast is so important, so beautiful. That's why Jesus ate this paschal meal with his friends for the last time.

"But this meal was a brand new meal, such as the apostles had never experienced before. It is the last Passover meal of the Old Testament. To be sure, everyone ate a part of the paschal lamb, but they all ate the food which Jesus gave them. They were united to him and to each other by means of it. Jesus took the bread and wine and gave thanks according to custom for gifts, and then he passed them to the apostles. But he said something new: 'Take and eat. This is my body. Take and drink. This is my blood.'"

"Mommy, he said that once before and the Jews became angry with him."

"Yes, he fed almost ten thousand people with five loaves and two fishes. After this unheard-of miracle, the people looked for Jesus. He knew they were looking for him and he said to them, 'Do not care for the food which passes, like bread and fish. Look for food which lasts forever, the eternal food which the Son of Man will give you.' 'Lord, give us this bread,' the people all cried. But when they heard the kind of bread he wanted to give them they didn't understand him any longer. On the contrary, they were disgusted. They thought that he was going against their customs. 'I am the living bread which comes down from heaven,' Jesus said. 'Whoever eats this bread will live forever. The bread which I shall give you is my flesh for the life of the world. Whoever eats my flesh and drinks my blood lives in me and I live in him.' 'What?' cried the Jews. 'He wants to give us his flesh to eat and his blood. We're not allowed to drink blood. It's in our laws. We're supposed to eat his flesh?' And they became angry and many disciples who believed in Jesus did the same. Jesus tried to quiet them, but they didn't understand. 'When the Son of Man goes back to heaven where he was before,' he said to them, 'then you will understand whose body it is you eat and whose blood you drink. It is the Spirit who gives life. The flesh does not matter. You will eat my transfigured body.' "

"Do we receive the transfigured body of Jesus to eat, Mommy?"

"Yes, and whoever eats this bread will never die because Jesus said, 'I am in him and he is in me.'

"Peter and the apostles were standing there too. The other disciples had gone away, but the apostles did not leave Jesus. 'Do you also want to go away?' asked the Lord.

"Jesus keeps asking you this question, too, —Isabel, Manuel,

Peter, Andrew, David, Daniel, Mommy, Papa: 'Will you go away, too?'"

"Is Jesus afraid that we'll go away, Mommy?"

"Afraid? No! But he keeps asking each one of us, 'Are you going away or are you staying with me? You belong to me. Are you listening to me? Decide for yourself. Answer me.' Peter answered, 'Lord, to whom shall we go? You are the only one we have. You have the words of eternal life, and we have believed and recognized that you are the Christ, the Son of God. We're staying with you, Lord, and we're going with you to the table and we are celebrating our new bond with you. You have said, 'This is my body which will be laid down for you. This is my blood, the blood of our new friendship, which will be shed for you and for many for the remission of sins. Do this in remembrance of me.'"

"Are we the many, Mommy?"

"We are the many. Tomorrow on Good Friday Jesus will give his life again and he will die on the cross. Tomorrow on Good Friday his blood will flow for the forgiveness of sins. He is the Easter lamb.

"That was the first Mass which we celebrate to this day just as Jesus commanded the apostles: 'Do this in remembrance of me.'"

"Did Judas receive holy communion?"

"We don't know exactly. If he did, he did it with an unworthy heart."

"But Jesus knew that. Why did he let him receive holy communion?"

"He did say, 'One of you will betray me.' And when Judas asked, 'Is it I, Lord?' Jesus answered, 'Yes, it is you. Do what you have to do quickly.' Perhaps Jesus only wanted to show what an unworthy communion is, a communion without sorrow, without love, without friendship with Jesus."

"These are the things we can't understand, Mommy."

"They are mysteries, not miracles. We don't understand them. We believe them. Each time we assist at Mass we show that we believe the words of our Lord."

Do we receive all of Jesus
in holy communion?

I would like to receive communion. Is David too young for this? David's understandable longing. The mother knows if her child is ready for holy communion. David is instructed in how to go to confession. Will the priest ever tell? The priest's duty to maintain secrecy. What shall I say? A child reviews his day. I'm loud because I want to show I'm angry. The reward motive. Recognizing the more subtle spitefulness of children. A child's small mistakes very important to him. Quarrels in the family. Examination of conscience. Teaching the child how to make a good confession. Who is the Son of God? Do I receive all of Jesus in holy communion? Departure from the notion that one receives only a part of Jesus. Mommy, I'd like to eat you. Turning away from God. When the yearning for Jesus begins to die. Evening Mass and David's communion. David and the other children in the family. A quarrel after communion. The "little demons." Belligerence. The reaction of many mothers to the notion of early communion. A child's faith. A mother can answer her child's questions. The roles of teacher and pastor. The child's father sets the example. The mother as first and most important teacher. A child wants to believe. The privilege of instructing a child. Let the little ones come to me, and forbid them not.

"WHY can't I go to communion now?" whispered David to me after the consecration at the Mass.

"I'll tell you later."

"But I already know everything!"

David looked at me questioningly but he remained silent. His mouth drew into a hard line. Once again the little hand forced its way into mine. "But we still have time!"

I wanted to laugh!

He looked at me seriously, turned away, and looked up at the altar. He didn't say anything further—how touchingly and childlike but how manfully he hid his disappointment. When I was going to communion, my conscience bothered me and I whispered to him, "I'm going for both of us, you and me."

"Yes," he answered, and no more.

Later I thought, "Isn't he right? He does know *everything* and doesn't he understand better than I do? Isn't his union with God more unhampered than mine is? What reason urges me to hold him back? O God, do I have a cogent enough reason? David is not supposed to receive holy communion because a child has to be in a certain school grade first. But why a certain grade? In some countries children receive holy communion when the parents and pastor decide that the child is ready. I was in a quandary. Our first four children had waited until the accepted age. O God, tell me what I should do! Shall I go according to what my reason dictates? Shall I go contrary to accepted custom? —But I'm David's mother and I know what he understands. I know that better than anyone else.

After Mass David said, "Mommy, but let me go with you the next time! Jesus is calling me, too, and I have to stay sitting in the pew. Mommy, say something. You said yourself I should be homesick for Jesus."

"Homesick? You mean longing for Jesus."

"That's the same thing. I really want to go."

Homesickness and longing change into desire. I made a firm resolution.

"David, this very afternoon I'm going to our pastor to ask him if he's not agreed that it's time for you to go to communion with me!"

"Do I have to go to confession, Mommy?" He was very excited but not at all worried.

"You'll have to go to our pastor, David, and he'll have a little talk with you to see if you know something about yourself and if you understand about God and his Son and the Holy Spirit. He'll also want to know how much you know about the Bible and then you'll make your first confession."

I didn't tell him that soon he would be subject to the commandments of the Church. This first confession ought to have the validity and meaning of a real first confession. It is the first time that a person speaks with his pastor about the things which up to now have been confided to the mother or kept by the child entirely to himself.

"Am I going alone?" asked David.

"All alone."

"Aren't you coming?"

"No, David, you'll do this all by yourself!"

"But I've done a lot of bad things."

"You've told God every night when you prayed that you were sorry. That's the important thing."

"Did you tell our pastor what I've done?"

"Of course not!"

"Not even a little bit?"

"Not even a little bit. The priest isn't allowed to talk about what people tell him when they go to confession. When the priest was ordained, that is, when he became a priest, he promised the bishop before everybody in the church that he would remain true to his office as servant of God and that he would obey the commandments of God. He'll never tell the slightest word which he hears in confession. He would rather have his tongue cut off."

"Mommy, the priest can talk only to God about the bad things I tell him, otherwise to no one else. You can always tell Papa or Grandmother."

"God has sealed the lips of the priest. He can never tell anything. He takes the place of God on earth because it's often easier for people to *tell* their sins, although sometimes it can be very hard. When a person is sitting there listening exactly to what people say, the people really have to think before they can say what they've done."

"How do I think, Mommy?"

"Just the way we do each evening when we go over the whole day together. You just have to remember which naughty things you keep repeating. For example, 'Every day after dinner I go noisily up the stairs to my room. I wake the baby up and then he starts to cry and becomes cranky.' "

"I stamp up the stairs because I don't want to take a nap and I show that I'm angry, Mommy."

"If you see that you do this every day then you can say, 'I've been disobedient, stubborn, and thoughtless every day. Every day the devil says to me, 'Now, David dear, just go nice and loud upstairs. Just you show them! Wake Daniel up! He'll give out a nice yell again! Go louder, more stubbornly. Slam the bathroom door closed. There! That's wonderful! You don't want to be better!' —That's the way the devil talks."

"But I don't like to go to sleep."

"But in spite of that you do go to sleep because you're tired. And what if you don't go to sleep?"

"Then I'm unbearable!"

"When you know that you can do better you should think about it and actually do better."

"I don't know if I want to."

"That's just it. The devil knows that, too."

"But I like to make noise when I'm cross. Then I get over it!"

"But if you have to take a nap every day, couldn't you think of something else? For example, 'I'm quiet. I'll go to sleep quickly' —and woops! it's time to get up! I'll reward you in order to help you. Before you go to sleep, you may feed the hens . . . !"

"Can I do it all by myself?"

"Yes, you may because I can trust you. . . ."

"Because I'm big?"

"Because you're big! Because you can think! Because you want to take your nap and because you already go to confession like a grown-up, like a person who thinks reasonably. . . ."

"What else shall I say when I think?"

"Now I'll play David. I will show you. Now pay attention! 'Did I have to hit Rudy? Was I really so hungry that I had to eat a third piece of corn, when it was really Manuel's? Did I really hide Rudy's book for the fun of it? I just wanted to see him hunt for it. I wanted to see him cry. He didn't have his book and so he couldn't do his work. Yes, that's just what

I wanted so that Miss Hiller would think he was a lazybones. And why didn't I want Rudy to do his work? So that she could praise me and say, "See, David did his work." And yesterday at prayer time I was nodding yes with my head and I was thinking about football and of how I was going to kick Peter in the stomach. I didn't pay the slightest attention. God doesn't have a bicycle; poor God! I know it's foolish, but I can make Isabel laugh when I say something like that. Yesterday I kept calling a naughty word beginning with a *b*. Rudy said it and I said it after him because he said it. I didn't finish my dinner today. I put carrots three times on a spoon and then let them fall slyly on the floor.' "

"Did you see me, Mommy? Nobody else saw it."

"Yes, I did, and later I picked them up and thought of the poor children in the Congo. They would gladly have eaten what you had left over. I thought of Lazarus and the glutton. . . ."

"But I wasn't hungry any more. . . ."

"Really? But you wanted some more meat!"

"I wasn't hungry for carrots any more."

"Just say, 'Mommy, I don't like to eat carrots.' Didn't I give you only a small serving?"

"Yes . . ."

"Isn't that being wasteful, especially for people who talk so much about hungry people? Listen some more. 'Sometimes I like to quarrel with my brothers and sister. I grumble.' Can't David say all this by himself?"

"Of course, I can." David was very impressed by my knowledge!

178

"And how would it be if I named a great big bad sin?" he continued.

"For example?"

"For example," and he thought very hard, —"something with killing or. . . ."

"That would be a lie."

"But Mommy, the other things are so stupid. They aren't a bit interesting for the priest."

"You're talking to the priest but it's really God you're talking to. It's Jesus who sits in front of you and listens. What would he say if you said something about killing just because you didn't want to bore the priest? You'll be talking with him just the way you talk with me in the evening, about what happened during the day. And if you don't know anything else to say just ask the priest to ask a question. Maybe he'll even ask you a few questions to see what you know about the Bible."

"Like what? Ask me a question."

"Well, he might ask you to tell him a miracle of Jesus or who was David in the Old Testament. Then tell him the way you do when we talk together. Perhaps you'll be able to tell him more than you tell me."

"Of course not, Mommy!"

"Yes, as you grow bigger you must try to do all this without my help. Then you'll be an independent man!"

My almost independent man went to the pastor, that is, I brought him to the door of the rectory and then left him. He came back very pleased!

"I knew all the questions, Mommy! There was just one which had two answers. The first one was about David and Goliath.

The next one was about Adam and Eve and then came the question with the two answers: Who is the Son of God?"

"And what did you say?"

"I said 'me.'"

For a few moments I was stunned by the rightness of this answer of which I had not thought.

"And what did the priest say?"

"He said that was right, but did I know who the Son of God, God's Son, was? Then I answered, 'You mean Jesus Christ? I know him well.'"

But David didn't say a word about his confession and I didn't ask.

In the evening, David said to me as he lay in bed, "Mommy, does a person receive all of Jesus in communion?"

"What do you mean?"

"Well, that people don't receive a leg or a little finger."

"No, of course not. I've already explained that to you. Jesus is not a little dwarf in the host. Jesus is in the host itself, and even if the priest gave you only one-fourth of the host you would still be receiving all of Jesus. It would be no punishment. How often have I been to Mass in a church somewhere and received only a small particle of the host so that everyone could receive holy communion?"

"Then why do we get such a big piece?"

"So that the priest can hold the host without letting it fall."

"Mommy, sometimes I'd like to eat you up just because I love you so much, just to have you all for myself, just to be so near you. Is that the way it is with Jesus?"

"It's a little like that because we must love him very much. We must long for Jesus. But you know, David, there are times when you also say, 'I don't want to see you again, Mommy, never again.' That's the way people act with God. They turn their backs on God. They don't have any more longing for him. They don't want him any more."

"And people have to wait until it comes back again, Mommy."

"Do you really believe that?"

"No," he answered meekly. "People just have to keep on praying even if they don't want to. Then their longing will come back. That's what you said. Is it really really true?"

"Yes, then they'll want Jesus again. You must ask God and thank him—above all—thank him."

"But today everything was beautiful, Mommy. I could feel it." David was very happy.

We all went with David to the next evening Mass. Our pastor thought a low Mass in the middle of the week would be just right. David was happy and peaceful. The other children got around him like a wall of protection. I whispered softly to him a few times: "Lord, have mercy—Holy, Holy, Holy—pray for the dead." "I'm so happy, Mommy," David said, and he went radiantly with us all to holy communion. He knelt, opened his mouth, and waited. I saw to it that he closed his mouth again and swallowed the host. He knew how the host was going to taste and he didn't have to wonder about it. I had given him an unconsecrated host to swallow a few days in advance.

"It doesn't taste at all," he said. Some children think they are going to have a heavenly taste and they are disappointed.

181

David went back to his place, and then looked up at the altar. He had taken so much in stride that I was very much moved and a bit excited. He whispered to me, "Don't look so sad, Mommy. Be happy!"

"I am happy!" He smiled at me confidently.

After the Mass the other children got around him and kissed him. They were so very proud of David. I had gotten a nice supper ready and the table was set. The children washed their hands and combed their hair. All of a sudden a quarrel was in progress! David was crying the loudest! "Now just stop it. Think about where you've all just been," I said.

Peace was immediately restored. Then Manuel said slyly and softly to me, "Mommy, I know what the matter is. It's the little demons after holy communion!"

"The little demons? What do you mean?"

"Well, the little demons, —the devils. I call them little demons. They always like to show up after church."

"You're right," I laughed. "I know that."

"Grown-ups are often in a bad mood after church," said Manuel.

That's right, too. I've noticed this about me and the children. I know this relaxing of tension. People give themselves over to all sorts of moods and irritations. That leads to unavoidable quarreling. I want to help the children control a situation like this. It is best, probably, to talk about it. I told them that I've been the victim of the little demons, too.

David wanted to sit near his father at table. Manuel gave up his place without a word and slid over next to me.

The children were happy again. Unfriendly words were at least "audibly" at bay.

The next day I met the mother of one of my pupils. "Don't you think that it's just too early for my Tony to go to communion with David?" she asked. Her boy was as old as David.

"No," I answered. "I should think that after a half year in the first class it's almost too late. These children have far-reaching faith and much more capacity for believing than we have.

"Everything you've taught your child since his birth prepares him to go to the table of God when he is five or six years old."

"But Tony understands absolutely nothing. He's not even going to school. The pastor or religion teacher can explain it all to him better than I can."

"That's not the way I think. The child is already accustomed to the way you say things. You talk with him and you answer his questions."

"Yes, but I just can't bring myself to telling him these difficult things. That's the reason for a teacher."

"No, that's for you, the mother. The teacher and the pastor can help out and explain further, but you're the best teacher for your child. You bear the responsibility and it's as great as your love for him. The faith of your child lives through your faith...."

"Yes, and the husband?"

"Through the faith of both parents! The father is the model. You are more with the child because of the circumstances of life. The child must know that you and his father are of the same mind. But tell me, what is it that your child doesn't understand?"

The woman became uncertain. "About grace, ... about sin, ... about the consecration," she murmured.

"Your child knows all about these matters. About his sins, —

183

they are for the most part only mistakes which you have daily talked over with him. And the consecration, —do you understand the consecration? I don't. I believe in it without reservation, sometimes tepidly, sometimes without adverting to it. The mystery itself cannot be understood completely. But the child stands there with his young heart and has no trouble believing. He is blissfully happy that Jesus is entirely in the host. For the child it is always a timeless today. He sits with Jesus at table and Jesus gives him food. The pure faith of the child, the unadulterated joy, power, yearning, directness—that is grace for the child. And what a grace it is for you when this child accompanies you to the rail! David said to me, 'After communion I'm so happy that I'd like to laugh, but too bad, I have to be serious!' I don't know if one should be so serious. Christianity is a happy religion. We seem to believe that happiness is incompatible with dignity. Haven't many of the saints smiled on their death bed?

"Weren't things serious for them? Sometimes I could laugh and cry at the same time because my heart is full to overflowing. What do you suppose happens in the case of our child? If you really believe in grace and in the power of God, then let the little one come to him and don't hold him back from him."

They could have rolled the stone away

What happened when Jesus died? Joseph of Arimathea and Nicodemus. The burial. Pilate places a watch at Jesus' grave. The resurrection. The women at the empty tomb. Mary Magdalen and Jesus. Thomas the apostle doubts the resurrection. Thomas later believes. We believe in Jesus without having seen him. Manuel sees Jesus.

"What was it like on the first Easter? Tell us about it before you read the story to us."

"After Jesus died a soldier came and pierced his side with a spear and blood and water flowed from the wound. The soldier saw that Jesus was dead.

"A secret disciple, a rich and distinguished man named Joseph of Arimathea, came to Pilate and asked for the body of Jesus. 'Is he already dead?' Pilate asked wonderingly. 'Take him.' Joseph got help from one of the other disciples, Nicodemus. He brought the good smelling woods which were ground and strewn between the linen swathing bands around the dead man, because decay sets in quickly in warm countries. It took about thirty pounds, which is as much as our Daniel weighs. They had to hurry with the burial because no one could be buried once the Sabbath had begun.

"Joseph and Nicodemus wrapped Jesus in winding bands and laid him in a cave in Joseph's garden which was very near Golgotha. You know that the hill on which Jesus died was called Golgotha.

"Then they gathered all their strength to roll a huge heavy stone at the entrance of the tomb.

"The Jews who had condemned Jesus were very angry with Pilate. 'Why did you give away the body of this criminal? Who knows what his disciples want with the body! They will steal it and then announce some miracle afterwards. Perhaps they may even say he is not dead.' Pilate wanted to quiet them so he placed a sentry, a centurion, at the door of the tomb. The guard stood there and did not allow anyone to come near."

"But Mommy, couldn't anyone roll the stone away?"

"But the centurion was on guard!"

"The disciples could have given him money or even held him."

"Yes, but then everybody would have known about it. Most likely a rope had been tied around the stone and some kind of seal affixed at the end of it."

"Just like Isabel! She's always stretching a string in front of her secret drawer so that she will know if anyone has been there."

"She puts it there because she doesn't trust you."

"Yes, she's right. We really do go in there!"

"A person is entitled to his secrets, Manuel. I never look in this drawer or in Andrew's closet!"

"Mrs. Melle says that a mother is supposed to know everything. She opens every one of her daughter's letters."

"So she does. But I think that isn't right. I have confidence in each one of you. Whenever you have anything which you don't want to show me, you have reasons which I respect. But let's go back to the centurion standing at the grave of Jesus."

186

"There was an earthquake, Mommy, and the sentry fell down on his face from fright. He acted like he was dead. And an angel rolled the stone away."

"How did he look, Peter?"

"I don't know because it was much too bright. He looked like lightning and had a very white gown on. . . ."

"Now the women who were often with Jesus came to the tomb. Up to now no one knew too much about them. They knew that the women were holy and very retiring, that they believed Jesus and loved him. 'Let's go to the grave,' they said."

"Martin visits his mother's grave every day," said Isabel. "So does Mrs. Till. She always visits Mark who was drowned and she brings him flowers from the lake."

"When the women arrived, the stone was already rolled away. One of the women, Magdalen, Mary Magdalen, entered the tomb and saw that it was empty. Greatly upset, she ran hurriedly to Peter and John. 'They've taken my Lord from the tomb and we don't know where they laid him,' she exclaimed.

"Peter and John went hurrying to the tomb. John arrived first so he looked into the tomb. The winding bands were lying neatly together. Peter now went in and John followed. They both believed that the Master had risen so they returned home.

"But Mary stood before the grave weeping. As she bent forward she saw two angels dressed in white garments sitting where Jesus had been. 'Why are you crying?' the angels asked. 'They have taken my Master away and I don't know where they have put him,' she answered. Just then she turned around and there was Jesus standing before her, but she didn't recognize him."

"But why didn't she if she had been with him so much and had loved him, too?"

"She couldn't see the glorified body of Jesus yet. Her eyes were held."

"Like the eyes of the disciples who were going to Emmaus?"

"Yes, they recognized Jesus only when he blessed them the way only he used to do. Mary Magdalen thought he was the gardener. But Jesus asked her the questions the angels did: 'Woman, why are you weeping? Whom are you seeking?'"

"But now she could know, Mommy!"

"No, not yet. Mary asked, 'Gardener, if you have carried him away, please tell me where you laid him because I want to get him.' Jesus said just one word: 'Mary!' No one had ever called her name in this way before. She turned to him, threw herself at his feet, and tried to embrace them, at the same time crying, 'Master!' Jesus spoke to her, 'Do not touch me. I have not yet gone to my Father. Go to my brethren and tell them I will ascend to my Father and your Father, to my God and your God.' Mary Magdalen rose and obeyed Jesus. Then she went to the disciples. The other women had also met Jesus, and falling on their knees they adored him. 'Go,' Jesus told them, 'go to my brethren. Tell them to go to Galilee and they will see me there.'

"Many people saw Jesus after his death. They talked with him and touched him. The women told the disciples how Jesus stood before them but they wouldn't believe the women."

"Why, Mommy? They all hoped that Jesus wasn't dead."

"They didn't have the strength. Think of Thomas. Even he didn't want to believe."

"He said it was women's talk," said Peter.

" 'If I do not see in his hands the place of the nails and place my hand in his side, I will not believe,' Thomas had said.

"A few days later the apostles were together and Thomas was with them. Suddenly Jesus stood in their midst and said, 'Peace be with you!' "

"He said that so often after he died," Manuel countered.

" 'Peace be with you. Place your finger here, Thomas. Put your hand here and place it into my side and be believing, not unbelieving.'

"Look at Thomas. He fell on his knees before Jesus and said full of happiness and contrition, 'My Lord and my God!' "

"Mommy, did he put his finger into the wounds?"

"No, when he saw Jesus he knew that the Lord had come. Jesus said, 'Because you have seen me, Thomas, you have believed. Blessed are they who have not seen and yet believe.' For example, you, David, or you, Peter, and all of you. You are blessed. You have not seen God but you believe."

"I have," Manuel chimed in. "When I was small I saw him often!"

"He's always seeing something," grumbled Peter.

Manuel was hurt. "But I've seen him, but I can't describe him."

"Let him alone. Small children see more than we think. God was certainly very close to Manuel."

"But blessed are they who . . ."

"Don't be heartless, Peter. God is here among us. We don't see him. He doesn't talk with us so that we can hear him with our ears. But we can sense that God is here. We know it and we believe it."

189

"Our Lord Jesus Christ is in the church. He is there when you visit him. He rose from the dead so that he could be with us all the time. 'I shall be with you all the time. I shall be with you even to the end of the world.' Lord, I believe in you, increase my faith."

But I know Jesus!

Andrew, Isabel's friend and counsellor. Andrew helps Isabel to get ready for confession. A child becomes self-reliant. Necessary weaning from the mother. Isabel at a Rembrandt exhibition. The disciples at Emmaus. Oh, you without understanding, how slow your heart is to believe. Lord, stay with us for it is evening. Isabel grasps the meaning of the picture.

I WENT to a Rembrandt exhibition with my little seven-year-old Isabel.

"You always take the boys with you. Girls ought to see something like that, too!" Her thirst for knowledge was very great. She wanted to know, to see, to have things explained to her, to learn. Andrew understood this very well and he accepted it very patiently. He read to her, showed her his lovely postcards, his art books, his rock collection. He played cards with her and they listened to music together. I'm very glad that he undertook to be responsible for her. In return, she gave him an unbounded confidence along with great admiration.

I shall never forget the day she said to me, "I'm going to confession today," adding casually, "Andrew helped me to get ready." She had done that with me formerly, but now she was already beginning to be self-reliant enough to ask Andrew to help her.

I considered her ability to wean herself from me a marvellous step forward. It was as satisfying as it was necessary.

These little steps into independence are natural and unavoidable. We should help our children to achieve them. New ties will be formed in this mother-child relation, new ones and stronger ones. Therefore, we should not be afraid to see our children become independent. So often I have become horrified when I saw how easily we and others tear down these structures. How often has this irritation with myself and with others been accompanied by impatience, words of a false moralism, lack of love and self control.

Today, then, we were at the Rembrandt exhibition. Isabel was indescribably proud and happy. We went into the first room. She walked silently and slowly from one picture to another gazing at each with attention.

"Do you know who that is?" I whispered to her as she stood before the aging Saul who was listening to young David as he played on his harp and sang.

She recognized the scene at once and was very happy about it. "Show me the ones I know!" Without any trouble she recognized Susanna and the three old men, Abraham and the three angels.

Then we came to the disciples at Emmaus. We took two chairs and sat down before the picture. I asked Isabel who the others were. She hesitated. "Jesus I already know, but I don't know who the others are."

"What are they doing?"

"They're sitting at a table."

"How do they look?"

192

"This is what they're doing," and she bent back and looked surprised.

"What are you doing, Isabel?"

"I was being surprised!"

"Are these men surprised?"

"Perhaps they're frightened, Mommy!"

"Do you remember Jesus' two disciples who were going from Jerusalem to Emmaus on Easter day? That's about six miles. They had been talking about Jesus and all the things which had happened during the week."

"Didn't they know that Jesus had risen?"

"No, they didn't know yet and they were very sad. While they were going along like this Jesus joined them and went along, too.

" 'What are you talking about?' Jesus asked them.

" 'Don't you know the things that have been happening in Jerusalem? Everyone knows about them. Jesus of Nazareth who was mighty in word and work before God and all the people was condemned to death by the people and he was crucified. We had hoped so much that he would redeem our people Israel. Several of our women have said that they have seen angels who said that Jesus is living. But we haven't seen him.' "

"Didn't they recognize him?"

"No, their eyes were held."

" 'Oh, you people of no understanding,' said Jesus. 'How slow is your heart to believe. Didn't Jesus have to suffer like this in order to enter into his glory?' And Jesus talked with them about all the things which had been said about him in the Scriptures."

"Who said?"

"The prophets!"

"Oh, I know! That's David, Daniel, Isaiah, . . ."

"All these prophets. As they were coming nearer to Emmaus the three looked at Jesus and said, 'Lord, remain with us, for it is evening.' Jesus followed them into the house which most likely belonged to one of the disciples and he stayed with them. As they were sitting at the table he took bread, blessed it, broke it, and gave it to them.

"Look at the picture, Isabel. Then their eyes were opened and they recognized him."

"So, that's the picture! They're just recognizing Jesus!"

"Then he disappeared from their sight.

"Imagine the picture without Jesus. See the disciples sitting in the dark and saying, 'Didn't our hearts burn within us as he was talking with us along the way explaining everything?'

"They went back immediately to Jerusalem where they wanted to find the other disciples to tell them that they had seen Jesus.

" 'Jesus is risen!' they cried out to them. 'Jesus is risen. Peter has seen him! We have, too,' —and then they told about what had happened on the road to Emmaus and of how they had recognized their Lord when he shared bread with them.

"Tell me, Isabel, tell me one thing which you remember from this event."

Isabel thought a while and then said, " 'Lord, remain with us, for it is evening.' " We looked at a few more pictures, but not too many more. At the end of the tour Isabel still wanted to go back to the Emmaus picture.

"Why, Mommy? So that I'll never forget it!"

194

I don't want to throw
my lunch away again

How do we hurt God the most? I took my little sister's lunch away from her and ate it. Hunger. The daily bread. Manna. Bread in the desert. Jesus under the form of bread. The miraculous multiplication of the loaves. Reverence for bread. Prayer at table. Love for grandmother. The lie. The deception. A dear departed person is always present.

"I WANT to tell you something, —you David, you Isabel. Manuel, you come here, too. Daniel may remain seated on his little bench."

"But he can't say a word!"

"That doesn't matter. He sees that he belongs to us and he senses that we belong together. And when we talk seriously among ourselves he behaves very quietly. Maybe he understands a little. I've prayed with each of you when you were in the crib."

"But we know that," said Manuel with assurance.

"Listen. Today I told the children in the school that they should try to think over what it is which displeases God the most. Is it an outburst of temper, or lying or something else? Each child was supposed to write his thought on a piece of paper without signing his name. Then we were going to talk

195

the matter over. But no one would be allowed to say, 'That's my paper. I wrote that!' Among the papers there was one which contained, 'When someone takes bread away from his little sister and then eats it'; 'when mother asked if I had already had bread and I answered no'; 'when I lied because I had already had two.' . . ."

"The child said that because he was hungry," said Manuel.

"You're right. It happened because he's always hungry. But look! See how well his conscience told him that he had taken bread away from his little sister. This child knows what bread is. It is the most desirable food. You, my children, you don't know this."

"We do! We like to eat breakfast!"

"Of course. But when you feel hungry you go into the kitchen and cut yourself some bread. When your hunger is gone, you leave the uneaten bread on the dish to get dry and perhaps to be thrown away."

"I give it to the chickens," confessed David frankly.

"But this child would never understand you."

"At school Susey always hides her bread under her apron. She takes a bite of it and then puts it back."

"God has given us bread. Look, I have here a grain of corn which was once a seed. When I grind corn it becomes flour, and bread comes from flour. But this bread does not last forever. Think of Moses in the desert with the people of God as they hungered and God sent them food which looked like bread, —manna. People sometimes don't like spinach, or meat, but everyone likes bread. A poor man begs for *bread*. Jesus gave us himself under the form of *bread*."

"At the miraculous multiplication of the loaves Jesus fed many with bread," said Isabel.

"He is the bread of life. And in the most perfect of all prayers, the prayer we say most often, we pray with Jesus, 'Give us this day our daily bread.'"

"I don't want to throw bread under the bushes any more. I won't ever do it again. I thought the birds would eat it but it stayed there," said Manuel. "No one may throw bread away just as long as one child is hungry."

"We have so much that we don't notice any more. . . ."

"Oh yes! We notice, but we don't understand this and we act without reverence. Thank you, dear Lord, for the bread which you have given us. During the war there was very little bread. People used to think with yearning about good bread."

"When you're away, Mommy, I miss you very much and I want you much more than when you're here."

"That's the way it is with bread. That's why we pray before meals just as the Jews were accustomed to doing and as Jesus did too."

Thank you, Lord, that you thought about us and that you fed us the way you did the people in the desert.

Give thanks to God because he is kind.

And his goodness endures forever!

At my Great Grandmother's every newcomer received bread and salt first.

"Did you love your Grandmother very much, Mommy? You speak so often about her. She's been dead a long time, hasn't she?"

"Well, not so long, six years. When David was seven months old she died. This was the saddest day of my life. I loved her more than anything else. My first drawings as a child always had my Grandmother in them. She was more beautiful to me than any other woman. She looked nice all the time and she was very careful about everything she did. Her room was always so tidy and pretty that she could receive guests there any time. She was never in a hurry, never ruffled. She never spoke too loudly. Yet she was always lively and gay. Her smile was perhaps the most charming part of her. She was gentle and had a natural dignity about her. It would never have occurred to me to speak loudly or to behave badly in her presence. When she praised me, I carried her praise like a banner before me for the whole day. I wanted to be like her in everything and I am so completely different."

"But you're pretty too!"

"A mother is always beautiful to her children, but Grandmother was something special. And because I loved her one day I lied brazenly to her."

"Oh tell us, Mommy!"

"You know, I knew how to use moulding material quite well and I made animals, flowers, and people. One afternoon, just for the fun of it, I covered my glass elephant with a coat of gray material just as Grandmother came in to see what I had been doing. 'What a lovely elephant,' she cried, enchanted. 'How beautiful! Did you perhaps make it for me? Are you going to give it to me?'

"At first I didn't want to deceive her. I really, really wanted to explain everything to her. But the happier she became the harder it was for me to tell her different. In the end, Grandmother left with my little elephant and she put it in her glass case. There it stood in the corner and she showed it to me. Whenever I came for a visit she always said, 'Don't you want to see your elephant? Each day when I look at it, it makes me so happy.'

"My bad conscience grew big, but my love for Grandmother was even bigger. As the years went by I could not bring myself to clear this matter with her. I'm thirty-five years old and still I haven't told her. . . ."

"You didn't want to tell her different, Mommy."

"No, I didn't, but I had no business lying to her either."

"But it made her so happy. . . ."

"I should have tried to make her happy with another gift. I was too vain and happy over my success. I revered her above everything and I trusted her more than anyone else. For this reason I should have had the courage. . . . Now she is dead. But she has remained alive in my memory. She is so alive that often I forget she is dead. I can't visit her any more but she is still loving and protecting me."

Did Jesus begin
only when he was born?

The true God. Is God something quite different? Uncertainty. Did Abraham, Moses, Gideon, David, and the others tell the truth? A child turns to God. Jesus is God. Jesus was always with God. Come, Holy Spirit, enlighten me. The disciples before Pentecost. The Ascension. Pentecost. The Holy Spirit and the apostles. The first confirmation.

I was very perplexed today when David who is now seven years old asked me suddenly and almost grieved, "Are you sure that we believe in the true God?"

I wanted to answer passionately, but I controlled myself and said very calmly, "Yes!"

"But, —if God is something different, Mommy! Perhaps people are imagining something not right."

"How do you picture God to yourself?"

"I don't know exactly. Just once in a while I think things."

"What sort of things?"

"That God is something quite different, that God wants to be something really different."

"But David, isn't there enough told us in the Bible by people like Abraham, Moses, Gideon, David, Daniel, and Job who believed in your God, who spoke with your God, and to whom God himself talked?"

"But maybe it was made up." David is visibly horrified at the mere thought.

"If you believe it could have been made up, do you believe in Jesus?"

"I believe in Jesus and in God, Mommy, I'm just asking . . ."

"Jesus, whom people were able to touch with their hands, whom they saw, this Jesus who cured them died and he rose from the dead, darling."

"Yes, I know. I used to be able to think better about God. Now I can think better about Jesus. I'm always thinking about Jesus."

"But Jesus is God, David. He was with the Father before the world was made."

"I keep thinking, Mommy, that he began only when he was born!"

"He was always with God just as much as the Holy Spirit. —David, I often pray to the Holy Spirit for his gifts. Come, Holy Spirit, and enlighten me that I may be able to give David the right answer. Come, Holy Spirit, give me strength that I may always have courage."

"You always have courage, Mommy!"

"No, I'm afraid often."

"In the night, Mommy?"

"No, not in the night. But, for example, whenever I come to someone's defense and must speak my mind before the people, I would much rather run away. Or, before talks when I see people in the hall I would rather turn around and go back home. Then I pray, 'Come, Holy Spirit, give me wisdom, counsel, strength, understanding, piety, and fear of God.'"

"Does he give you all that?"

"He gives me what he sees is necessary for me. Look at the

apostles at Pentecost! Jesus had risen from the dead and they were waiting for the Holy Spirit because Jesus had promised him to them before he left them."

"You mean, before he went back to heaven?"

"Jesus had kept his promise. He had died and arisen. He had lived again and people had seen him, talked with him, touched him, and eaten with him.

" 'I shall not be with you much longer. I am returning to my Father. My Father is your Father. My God is your God. I shall never leave you. I shall remain with you forever, until the end of the world.'

"And then he went with his disciples to Bethany, looked up to heaven, blessed them, and as he was blessing them, he was taken up into heaven from their sight. The disciples fell down and adored him. Afterwards they stood up, happy and joyful. They often sat together behind locked doors because they were afraid of the enemies of Jesus. They waited and prayed. One day a great wind suddenly filled the room and fire came down from heaven. It parted and remained hanging like many small tongues of fire over the heads of the disciples. And just as suddenly as the fire had come down from heaven, just so suddenly did the whole life of each one present change. Now they were no longer afraid. Their hearts were full of love for Jesus, and words came from their lips which had not occurred to them before. They threw open the doors, went out into the street, and talked to everyone they met about God. They knew what to say. They were wise and reasonable and what they said went directly to the hearts of the people. Much more, these poor ignorant fishermen spoke languages which they had never learned.

"Imagine how surprised everyone was. The people were so

astonished, so impressed and excited, that many of them received baptism and believed in God. And the apostles laid their hands on these newly baptized people, strengthening them with the Holy Spirit who was in them. That was the first confirmation. You, too, will be confirmed some day. The bishop will come and he will lay his hands on your head and pray to the Holy Spirit to come down on you and make you strong for the whole of your life."

"And does he do it, Mommy?"

"Yes, he does."

Did Mary see the angel?

Hail, Mary, full of grace! The biblical account of the Annuncia-
tion. God is born. God allowed himself to be crucified. The
mystery of the Trinity. Mary's obedience. I am a handmaid of
the Lord. May it be done to me according to your word. Mary
goes to Elizabeth. Elizabeth is also expecting a child. Elizabeth
is filled with the Holy Spirit. Mary, the mother of my Lord,
comes to me. Magnificat. *Litany.*

"WHEN I say the Hail Mary, *I'm* the angel every time," said
Manuel.

"When you really greet Mary, you are like the angel and she
is full of grace. She is blessed among women. She alone, she and
the fruit of her womb, Jesus, are blessed."

"Mommy, did she really see the angel with her own eyes?"

"Yes, the angel came to her. But I'll just read the story from
the Bible to you. It's so beautiful that you'll be able to understand it without any trouble."

". . . the angel Gabriel was sent from God to a town in Galilee
called Nazareth, with a message for a girl betrothed to a man
named Joseph, a descendant of David; the girl's name was Mary.
The angel went in and said to her, 'Greetings, most favoured
one! The Lord is with you.' But she was deeply troubled by

what he said and wondered what this greeting might mean. Then the angel said to her, 'Do not be afraid, Mary, for God has been gracious to you; you shall conceive and bear a son, and you shall give him the name Jesus. He will be great; he will bear the title "Son of the Most High"; and the Lord God will give him the throne of his ancestor David, and he will be king over Israel for ever; his reign shall never end.' "

"The angel greeted Mary with great reverence just as he would have greeted the queen of the angels, because she was full of grace in the sight of God, because God had selected her to be his mother."

"Why do you say *his* mother? She is supposed to be the mother of Jesus and Jesus is the son of God, isn't he?"

"Yes, but Jesus is also God and the Holy Spirit is also God. All three Persons are one God. That's a mystery, a divine mystery that people can only believe without understanding it quite."

"But Mommy, God came into the world then and he let himself be crucified?"

"God in Jesus, his Son. God became man. We say it this way, 'And the Word was made flesh.' "

"I almost understand, Mommy."

"We know that God the Father, God the Son, and God the Holy Spirit are one God. But it remains a mystery and we can only say yes to it the way Mary did. Do you think she understood everything that happened to her? She knew only that God wanted it this way and that she wanted to obey. She asked how it was all going to happen. The angel answered her with words just as hard to understand, but they reassured her so that she accepted the incomprehensible. Nothing is impossible to God. Look, her cousin Elizabeth was expecting a child although she was old and should in no way have been expecting a child. But God can do all things. Mary, the little Mary, said very calmly because she wanted what God wanted and because she loved God very much, 'I am a handmaid of the Lord. Be it done to me according to your word.' Mary wasn't proud. She said humbly before God, 'Do with me what you will. I will obey, O my God. I want to be the mother of the redeemer. I look forward to my child, to my Jesus.' Jesus means: God is the redeemer. —'I look forward to my child.' And the angel left her.

"Then in greatest secrecy Mary started off to visit her cousin Elizabeth. She kept recalling the visit of the angel to her and she thought in her heart about each word the angel had spoken. She hurried to Elizabeth who lived in a city of Judah.

"This was real far away· She would certainly have to be five days on the way before she would reach the house of her relatives Elizabeth and Zechariah. Listen to what the Bible says."

"About this time Mary set out and went straight to a town in the uplands of Judah. She went into Zechariah's house and greeted Elizabeth. And when Elizabeth heard Mary's greeting, the baby stirred in her womb. Then Elizabeth was filled with the Holy Spirit and cried aloud, 'God's blessing is on you above all women, and his blessing is on the fruit of your womb. Who am I, that the mother of my Lord should visit me? I tell you, when your greeting sounded in my ears, the baby in the womb leapt for joy. How happy is she who has had faith that the Lord's promise would be fulfilled!' "

"When Mary greeted her cousin putting her arms around her, the child in Elizabeth's womb moved and she was filled with the Holy Spirit. She sensed the nearness of the redeemer and spoke like a prophet. 'How does it happen that the mother of my redeemer comes to me?'

"She knew that Mary was expecting a child. She sensed it and the Holy Spirit said to her, 'You are blessed because you have believed what was said to you by the Lord.'

"Mary knew too that she would have a child. And Mary sang her thanks to God in a most beautiful prayer. I've read it to you often and you can surely say it along with me. Mary spoke in great humility and overwhelming joy. She thanked God. She knew that Christians would always call her blessed.

" 'God has mercy on us,' she sang, 'the great God has mercy on his people Israel.' "

Mary, all generations will call you blessed!

Manuel, David, Andrew, Isabel, Peter, Daniel, fathers, mothers, —we bless you.

You, O Mother of Christ!

Mother most wonderful!

Mother of our redeemer!

Mother most pure!

Cause of our joy!

Mystical rose!

Morning star!

Gate of heaven!
Queen of angels!
Queen of all saints!
Queen of peace!
Our mother!
Pray for us.

"Jesus loved his mother so much. How happy he must be when we praise his holy mother, when we bless her, call her by the most beautiful names, when we trust her and ask her to pray for us."

O kindest of mothers, ask your Son to give us the strength to be obedient as you were.

Yes, Lord, I come. I obey. I give up fighting with Peter. You are asking it, Lord.

May your dear mother help me.

You shot at people?

Papa's war injury. The Russians are bad, Papa, they shot you during the war. I shot too. War. Death and murder. David limps. Identifying with a beloved father.

"WILL you go hiking with us, Papa, when we take our trip?"

"Of course I will. There's nothing I like better."

"But you can't walk too long with your leg, can you, Papa?"

"I do limp, but I can walk very well because I wear orthopedic shoes."

"Why do you always say that you get them from the state?"

"Because everyone who was injured in the war receives compensation from the state. I get shoes for my short leg, do you understand?"

"Did you see the Russian who shot you?" David wanted to know.

"No, the shot came from a tank."

"How many times?"

"Seven shots . . ."

"Did you cry, Papa, when you were lying there?"

"No, but I was sad to have to die—sad on account of my mother, my grandmother, sad because I had no children and I wanted children so much."

"Did it hurt a lot?"

"I was very numb. I lay as if in a half sleep. Sometimes the hours passed very quickly."

"The Russians are bad because they *shot* you."

"No, the Russians aren't bad for that reason. I shot, too."

"You shot, too?" Isabel was horrified.

"Yes, I shot, too."

"At people or in the air?"

"At people; that is, I shot in their direction. We were soldiers in a war."

"That's terrible. I would never have dreamed that you shot, too."

"Yes, I know. I think war is terrible, too. . . ."

"But you killed people," broke in Isabel while her father was still talking.

"Do you know the difference between murder which took place between Cain and Abel and killing in war?"

"No," said Isabel. "It's just plain killing."

"But it is something different when one thinks that both sides, the Russians and the Germans, were standing opposite each other shooting at each other, both sides knowing well what was going to happen."

"There have always been wars," said Andrew, "in the Old Testament, after Christ, in the Middle Ages, all the time."

"I don't want Papa to go shooting any more," said Isabel sadly. "I don't want that any more."

We were three weeks with the children in the mountains, and the many walks and hikes with father were a great joy for them. I remained in the cabin with Daniel because he was still too small. The days were delightful and the children returned home strengthened and browned.

Three days after we got home it seemed to me that David was dragging his right foot. I watched him for a while. He actually was doing just that!

"Does your leg hurt, David?"

"No, Mommy."

I let him skip over a rope. He limped. I let him jump down from a chair and he favored his right leg. I became somewhat apprehensive. After two days the situation had not bettered itself so I took him to the doctor. He was X-rayed for atrophy of the muscles and otherwise thoroughly examined. The doctor found nothing the matter. Still David limped.

We were faced with a riddle. After fourteen days of the greatest anxiety David himself gave me the key to the puzzle. He said to me, "I love Papa so much that I want to be just like him, —just as big, same kind of glasses, same hands, everything, everything!"

Suddenly I asked him, "And to walk like Papa? Do you want to do that, too?"

"Yes, Mommy, I want that, too."

Very patiently I explained to my David that he could be like Papa but that he didn't have to limp. It turned out that David had always walked behind his father when they were going along the mountain paths. David had identified himself with his father to the extent that he wanted to imitate him absolutely in everything.

Two days later David was walking again without limping. My friend Barbara wanted to know if that wasn't dissimulation. But I tried to make it clear to her that it was no dissimulation. It was the wish to be like someone David loved very much.

What power lies deep in a child and how he can misuse it! David undid the work of his own doing without shock, without infringement on him, and without force.

Tell us about paradise

*What is Advent? Tell us about paradise, Mommy. Security and
happiness in paradise. The command. Adam wants a companion.
Eve. The first marriage union. The serpent, the devil. Adam
and Eve disobey. Shame, abandonment, fear. God's punishment.
The husband will have to work hard. The women will bear
children in labor. God gives the first people the hope of salvation.
Advent is this hope. We make an advent wreath. Singing. God
has pity on the first people. God comforts us too.*

"What is Advent, Mommy, I mean the word?" asked Andrew.

"Advent is the time before Christmas," said Peter.

"Advent is dark with just one light and then more and more,"
added Manuel.

"Advent," explained Isabel, "is Joseph and Mary in the night,
in the Old Testament. They were waiting for the birth of the
redeemer. He was the light of the world. When he came the
darkness went away." How I liked Isabel's answer.

"Advent means coming!"

"Tell us about paradise, Mommy!"

"Did Adam have to work, Mommy?"

"Adam had to work. He had to till the garden of paradise.
He had to make the land produce something."

" 'Work in my garden the earth,' said God the Father.

" 'Tend my garden the earth,' he said further.

"Maybe God meant the devil when he said that. Adam must be cautious of him. The work was easy and everything Adam did was a success."

"There was no hail, Mommy," said Manuel, who had a horror of catastrophes in nature.

"No, no hail, no lightning. . . ."

"No war?" asked Manuel again.

"No, no war. In paradise there was only joy and peace. Everything grew beautifully. The trees bore fruit. The seeds came up. There were thousands of flowers which bloomed, scattered seed around, and bloomed again. Adam was the steward of a large property on which everything turned out right. He had no worries."

"Yes, he did," said Peter. "There was the command. A command is always hard."

"For Adam it wasn't so hard as it is for you. His heart was without darkness and fear. Adam was happy but alone."

"I don't understand that," said Andrew. "If he was in paradise and belonged to God, how could he have been alone?"

"Maybe he wanted somebody to play with," said David.

"Or someone to tell things to. He couldn't share his happiness with anyone. . . ."

"Why didn't he talk to God?" Andrew wanted to know.

"Because he loved God very much. He respected him and didn't want to disturb him."

"That's right!" agreed Andrew.

"Adam was tremendously grateful to God when he gave him a partner."

"Where did the partner come from?" asked Peter.

"God gave her to Adam. Eve was now a part of him and they belonged to each other. So they wanted to live together and this was the first marriage union."

"Like Papa and Mommy."

"Yes, just like you later. You'll leave us some day to live with a man or woman!"

"We read in the Bible that Adam and Eve ate the fruit of the tree of knowledge."

"The snake deceived her."

"Did she have to disobey God? Wasn't she happy in paradise?"

"But it was the devil," snarled Peter. "It was the devil under the form of a serpent. The devil hated God because he was one of the fallen angels. He wanted everything that God didn't want."

"The fallen angel is very clever. How easy it was for him to make Eve curious, to catch her unawares, to tempt her. How easily we let ourselves be tempted."

" 'What is it about this fruit? What is going to happen to me on account of it? What is death and life? What is death?' asked Eve. 'Eat the fruit,' said the evil one. 'Nothing bad will happen to you.'

"And just as soon as Eve had eaten the fruit she gave some to Adam. Both were disobedient to God who had been so good to them. They seemed not to stand in awe, but they were only curious. When Adam and Eve heard God approaching they looked at each other in horror. They had not obeyed God. Because they saw each other naked they were ashamed. It was a completely new feeling."

"I dream something like that, Mommy. I dream I'm going to school with only a shirt on and it's much too short."

"These are the feelings Adam and Eve had. They were ashamed and they covered themselves before God's gaze. This was their way of admitting that they had been disobedient."

"And they were afraid, too. Adam said, 'Eve gave me the fruit.' Eve blamed the serpent."

"That's true. That's the way it was." Neither one wanted to be blamed. And then God punished them."

"Yes, Adam would have to work from then on. . . ."

"He had to do that before all this happened, Peter, but now he will do it only with difficulty. It will be hard to get things to grow. He will have to exert himself. Things will not go right for him. Things done without hard work in the garden of paradise became only a memory now.

"And Eve will bring her children into the world in anguish. She will bring them up with trouble, educate them with endless worries until they leave home to begin a family of their own.

"So Adam and Eve were sent out of the garden and now a life of sorrow began for them. How often they must have thought about their life in the garden of paradise, about the time they had the light. But God gave them a hope which we understand better than they did: You will be reconciled with me. I will give you the strength to overcome the devil. Between you, Eve, and the devil, I will set up an enmity. Between your children and the devil I shall set up an enmity. Eve, you became a friend of the serpent, but I know that you are sorry; therefore I will help you in your fight against the evil one. I will help you, your children—that you may all come out of the battle victorious. That was the hope. It was a small ray of light. That is Advent."

"Advent, Mommy, that's Advent! And the birth of Jesus is the light! Everything belongs so much together, Mommy!"

"Now let's make a nice big Advent wreath with candles. Where is the wire and the purple ribbon? Where are the candles? Tomorrow we will light the first candle of hope and we will sing."

"What are we going to sing?"

"Advent songs: 'Lift up your gates,' and 'There comes a ship a-sailing,' and 'Wake up! comes the voice of the watchers to us from high on the battlements. Wake up, Jerusalem!' —That's my favorite song!"

"I want to ask you something all alone, Mommy."

"What, then?"

"Did the animals become angry because Adam and Eve were afraid of them all of a sudden?"

"Because Adam was no longer the master of creation. Because of his sin he became helpless. He became subject to death and he lost his liberty. The animals sensed this."

"Do you know what I think is very nice? God himself made clothes for Adam and Eve!" said Manuel.

"Why do you think that's so nice?"

"Because he pitied them. He saw that they were ashamed. And if you are sorry for me you are no longer angry with me. Then you wipe my nose and help me to pull up my trousers. That makes me happy even if I was a little bad."

"But that has nothing to do with Adam and Eve," the older brother called out loudly. He always had to speak his mind!

"For me it does have something to do with it," I said "I

don't tell you fairy tales. Manuel has rightly applied this to himself."

"Clothes made of skin are wonderful," said my little David conciliatingly.

Later in the evening I sat alone and thought. Another liturgical year was beginning and with it new questions, new opinions by the children. Their demands will be harder and more pressing. Their consciousness will be more acute. It is good so. It means that God does not burden a person with more than he can endure at one time. May he give me the answers my children will need.

Index

219

220

375.2
Db39

69113

AUTHOR Becker, Antoinette

TITLE Children ask about God and everything.

ROOM

375.2
Db39

Date Due 69113

DEMCO NO 295

DE 1 4 '66				